"Sex is rampant in thi
fashion; it sells everythii
friends don't always give the best advice. But what does
the little three letter word really do to us and inside of
us? Written in a conversational, girlfriend to girlfriend
tone, *Inside of Me* is a poignant, engaging and realistic
book that will not only help save your life and protect
your heart; but also save your soul. Shellie Warren has
done an outstanding job keeping it real while keeping
you turning the pages. I highly recommend it for those
you care about, too." —Marina Woods, Founder,
goodgirlbookclubonline.com

"Her book is the *Waiting to Exhale* for not only
younger sisters, but young brothers … Besides being
full of detail that overflows with emotion, Shellie's
writing is clear and fluid—simply a wonderful read.
Without question, she is a talented writer. While this
book is her first, it is unlikely to be her last."
—Lucas Johnson II, author of *Finding the Good*

"*Inside of Me* is a victory! And for this, I applaud
Shellie. I am very proud of this lady who is now on
the other side of healing and invites those like herself
who have suffered, to step out on faith and reach for
the Master's hand. May the light continue to surround
her and grace ignite every step she takes. Continue to
enlighten and teach us, Shellie." —Hattie Winston,
actress, singer, writer

"While this may appear to be a book for woman
and sexuality, the male population will find this one
woman's story more than insightful. Ms. Warren, I am
positive, will be applauded for her courage, humility
and faith." —James M. Lisbon, Founder, AMAG/
Awareness magazine

inside

of me

lessons of lust, love and redemption

shellie r. warren

Inside of Me:
Lessons of Lust, Love and Redemption
By Shellie R. Warren
Relevant Books

Published by Relevant Books
A division of Relevant Media Group, Inc.
www.relevantbooks.com
www.relevantmediagroup.com
© 2004 by Relevant Media Group

Design: Relevant Solutions
Mark Arnold, Joshua Smith
www.relevant-solutions.com
Relevant Books is a registered trademark of Relevant Media Group, Inc., and is
registered in the U.S. Patent and Trademark Office.

For information or bulk orders:
RELEVANT MEDIA GROUP, INC.
POST OFFICE BOX 951127
LAKE MARY, FL 32795
407-333-7152

Library of Congress Control Number: 2004092068
International Standard Book Number: 0-9746942-2-3
04 05 06 07 9 8 7 6 5 4 3 2 1
Printed in the United States of America

To the ones who gave me life, M. Eugene Warren and Gail Masondo; the ones who gave me love, (the late) Damien A. Bell and W. Fredrick Holt; and the One who gave the gift, Jesus Christ, the Author and Finisher.

foreword

One thing I have learned is that nothing makes pain worse like holding it in. There's a voice that tells us that it would be best to let it out and let it go, but fear in all it myriad forms speaks louder, (or is it just easier to pay attention to?)

Fear says, "What will people think of me if they knew I did these things or that these things were done to me?" Fear says, "I'm too embarrassed to even admit to myself, let alone this man that I'm trying get to love me, that my life ain't perfect, that my body ain't perfect, that I ain't perfect." Fear masquerades as strength. We tell ourselves, "I'll just forget about it," " I'm over it," and probably the biggest untruth of all, "I don't care."

All the while the pain has been sitting somewhere in our bodies so long that we get used to walking, talking, sitting, standing, dressing, relating, eating, LIVING, in a way that medicates our hurt. Just like medicine only treats the physical symptoms, Fear doesn't heal it only treats the emotional symptoms.

The irony of this situation is that it takes courage to be vulnerable; it takes strength to accept your weaknesses. It takes guts to really, I mean REALLY dig deep, see, accept, and LOVE yourself.

Inside of Me: Lessons in Love, Lust and Redemption is both a powerful voice and a powerful tool for those of us in the process of releasing fear and learning to love again. I believe this book gives a voice to those who haven't yet found their own. Even if you can't put your words together just yet, the universe hears you. This book reveals that none of us are alone in are experiences of sexual abuse, and "misuse."

Inside of Me shows us that inside every lesson there's

a blessing, and most importantly that God loves us all just the way we are and we should love ourselves too.

One thing I've learned through song writing is that nothing eases pain like embracing it, blessing it, and expressing. We can make the decision, no matter how far gone we may think we are to change our lives and walk, talk, dress, eat, relate, love, and LIVE in ways that draw to us the energy of wholeness and healing into our lives.

Shellie Warren's daring to tell a story she is not far removed from is inspiring to me and it is my prediction, (just as Shellie predicted in my very first interview EVER!) that her words will touch many others as well.

It is my hope that this story will move all who read it to hear past fears whispers to Love's bold and beautiful song. To live in love is your divine right.

Strength, Courage & Wisdom,
India.Arie

acknowledgements

I want to first take the time to thank God, for always being true to His Word. Thank You for trusting me enough to let me write such a personal book that I know will be a powerful tool used in Your kingdom.

My mother, for appreciating and supporting my talents before I ever did and for trusting enough in God's forgiveness to allow me to use my past to help those in present need. I love you. It is finished.

To her husband, Victor Masondo, for being a part of God's restoration plan as it relates to the lives of my family. You are awesome.

My brother Jonathan Christian and "Zion" to some — you have mind-boggling talents. I can't wait to see what God has in store for you and your music. In the meantime, know that you will always be star that shines heads above the rest to me. Thank you for always being one of my best friends. I love you much.

Thank you, W. Fredrick Holt, for being the kind of man who did not need to be a character in this book. I know it has taken a lot for you to swallow your pride and support me in such a revealing endeavor. Thank you for seeing who I am rather than who I used to be and for loving me in a way that I believe God does — without reservation or apology.

To Lisa Kimmey, Marilyn Cathey, Anastasia Nocentelli, Angie Hinds (we'll keep the "C" word between us), Sandy BeCoats, Shauna Randolph, Marina Woods, Cole Warren, Rachel Hockett, Lisa Jordan, Ms. Neise, Sharon Johnson, Hattie Winston, Jean Wilson, Carrie Ferguson, and Carmen Starling — my sistahs, my family — thank you for always supporting me, loving me, and believing in me even when I didn't support, love, or believe in myself.

If I ever make some real money, I am taking us all on a cruise—well, after I buy a new car!

To Brian Jones (both of them), James Randolph, Floyd Boykin, Jr., Lee Clemmons, Derek Mason, David Wilson, Mario Nocentelli, Michael Chester, Dexter Conner, Gerard Gold, Keithie (in Philly), Christopher Davis, Church, Khari B., Tri Taylor, Duawne Starling, Terry Williams, Stacy Jones, Harold Wheeler, Anthonol Neely, Monte Lester, Moses Olomo, Stanley Fields, and Marquis Foxx— thank you for being healthy male friends who were always available for much needed advice or a shoulder to cry on. And thank you for knowing how to be "just friends" with a woman. It's a lost art.

To those who have helped me on the journey toward this book and beyond—first of all, to the RELEVANT staff for being open to such a radical project and for giving me the opportunity in your revolutionary magazine as well. Also to Teresa Hairston (who published my first personal narrative), Rosetta Miller-Perry (who published my first news piece), Trenay Perry Bynum, Lucas Johnson, Tyora Webbin, Morris Tipton, K. Danielle Edwards, Kendra Story, Tim Ghianni, Sandy Smith, Shane Olsen and Dwann Holmes Olsen, "b-gyrl," Carla Underwood Hamp, Kristin Whittlesey, Paula Major, Bonnie Newman, James Threalkill, Nashon Fondren, Jay Swartzendruber, Leah Follis, Debra Lawson, Maria Dowd, Denene Millner, Chris Jackson, Erica Jones, LaConia Jenkins, James Lisbon, Ron and Demetrus Stewart, Steve Benson, Gloria Anglion, and the hosts of others whose names I may have forgotten because unfortunately, I do not keep all of the clips of my work. Also thank you to those on the email ministry list who consistently send me encouragements, especially Carla J. Curtis. At times, I have needed them more than you will ever know, and I am eternally grateful for the seeds you have planted into my life.

To the seasonal people in my life who were there to cover me in the some of the coldest times I've ever had — Paul and Lynesa Benson, LaToia Crozier, Marcella Watts, Kathy Beagles, Chuck Stanford, Vicki Sewell, Kelli Williams, Kevin Ashmeade, Sarah Gaines, Lizzette Churchwell, Jade Gaje, Ingrid Owens, Noelle Kirkham, Stephanie Rankin, Claudia Harmon, Isaac Conner, Martha Bell, Lara Thurmond, Hope Anding, Christopher Jackson, Cynthia Chea, Chrystalyn Burnett (for being the first person to pray with me when Damien died), Meeka Winn, Steve Norman, the Chaffee Family, the Brown Family, the Bell Family, the Cathey Family, the Baker Family, and those I may have inadvertently overlooked because I have had more drama in my life than I would care to remember. Thank you.

To the myriad of people who either unknowingly or consciously planted a seed (whether it be an encouraging word, a monetary gift, or a prayer) into my life. Your harvest is on the way!

To those who had "ill intentions" — whether in word or deed — that were meant to tear me down. Your rudeness made me more resilient. Perhaps, I thank you most of all.

And finally, to all of the characters who played a role in this saga — although your names have been omitted (for obvious reasons), I want to thank you for the lessons learned, and I also want to take this time to formally apologize for any part that I played in the mess. This is my way of cleaning it up and throwing it out for good. So let it be written. So let it be done.

table of contents

introduction

Approximately one year before I entered my twenties, I started having sex. Ironically, approximately one year before I exited my twenties, I was given the opportunity to share some of my experiences with you, which is what *Inside of Me* is all about. If you think this is some religious rigmarole about sex, think again. I think sex is a beautiful thing, and even now as a single woman, it is only my daily relationship with God and the faith in someday being able to do it in the best setting—a marital one—that I am finding the strength to do without it. I am wise enough to know now that without Him, I will fall, but I am also wise enough to know that in having sex my way rather than God's way, falling and failure are inevitable. Even if you have been dating someone for years, or even if you married the person with whom you were sexually active as a single person, there are relentless prices to pay that are often more than a struggling couple can afford. But it doesn't have to be that way, and that is what I am hoping my story will help you to avoid.

I won't lie to you. Like a person dieting from sweets, once a sexually active person commits to a life of abstinence, major self-control is required. The reality is, like the sweets, sex is great, but when it is abused (abnormally used), it can be deadly, because it can severely affect everything about you—from your self-image and physical health to your present relationship with God, as well as the ones with your future spouse and children.

Sexual misuse (sex used outside of God's intention),

like so many other things in life, has the promising potential to be very hazardous to your spiritual, physical, and emotional well-being. The fact is, anytime you use anything to fill the voids in your life (whether it be food, dieting, drugs, drinking, work, money, image, power, people, and yes, sex), you will have a tendency to abuse (abnormally use) it, because you are dealing with the symptoms rather than the real problem. Here are some of the signs that you are using sex as a curse rather than a gift: If you are having sex to maintain a dating relationship; to raise your self-esteem; to distract you from your past; to be like everyone else; to please someone else (at the expense of your safety and happiness); to temporarily avoid your problems in life; or out of habit, addiction, or impatience. If you are using sex in any of these scenarios, it is guaranteed that in some way, sex will leave you worse off and emptier than before you started having it, because the purpose of sex is to celebrate an already-established, committed relationship, not to solidify or create one; prayer, time, and verbal communication does that. Trust me when I say that I've had first-hand experience, so I would know.

If you don't believe me, keep reading.

laying her to rest

I stand here and weep because
I miss and mourn what used to be
Not so much the lifestyle but the familiarity
Since birth you've been all I know, all I see and my reality
Believing that how you were was
how I was meant to be, my destiny
But you never could and I can say no longer will be
You had moments you impressed the masses,
you seemed to be so charming
And in spite of your mistakes and trials,
you were so strong seemingly
You gave to others unrestrained
yet somewhat co-dependently
Which explains why you played the victim,
physically and mentally
And because you did not prize your value,
you portrayed worthlessness spiritually
Which led to outbursts of pain and sickness emotionally
Trying to be everyone's friend and always your own enemy
Longing to be loved so you gave up your virginity
Seeking for approval so you ended every pregnancy
Never knowing God but claiming Christianity
Lacking self-esteem, longing for some level of vanity
For years this would be the cycle, dancing with the enemy
Making love to his imps while he planted seeds of enmity
That harvested mass confusion, choking your creativity
Leaving you without support and without any family
Believing all was well, but your life was ending terminally
You exhausted all your usefulness,
your influence becoming damaging
Appointed yourself as a whore,
when a queen is what you were called to be
Who knew to become royalty that
you had to be the death of me?
I stand here mourning the loss of the woman that I used to be
Not cloaked in dreary black but in the whiteness of purity
Not denying I am fearful for you were my identity

But we have nothing in common,
your rebellion hinders my ministry
I've revived you a time or two,
not ready for you to leave me
But my as soul was getting stronger,
you were steadily weakening
And as you took your last breath,
I inhaled life refreshingly
With it you took your past, your friends,
and they are now my history
And as in any death, I know you can't return to me
But like every life, I will cherish every memory
You have set the standard of the person
I don't want to be
Who knew to truly live,
you had to be the death of me?

© Shellie R. Warren, 2001

chapter one
inside my beginning

I planned on being a virgin on my wedding day. Well, that's mostly true. The real truth is that while I wasn't sure if I could wait long enough to boldly wear white as I walked down the aisle, I definitely did not intend on knowing more than one person intimately— figuratively, literally, or biblically. Have you ever heard what they say about the road to hell? Let's just say that intentions simply aren't good enough.

See, because I came from a long line of divorcers and divorcees, unlike many of my Christian private school peers with whom I attended high school, I had no intentions of exchanging my cap and gown for a veil and bouquet immediately following graduation; this meant that my physical desires, which I was told were natural, had to be put on reserve until I met and married "the one." That was the way I was taught, and so that is what I believed. But when it came to sex and relationships, that was about all I knew for sure until about a year before I decided to write this book. Up until now, I thought I was mature enough to handle a lot of what I'm about to share with you. Age—no matter how legal you may think it makes you—isn't everything.

I know, I know. There is something mind-boggling about being eighteen. Suddenly you think that just because you can vote, you are mature enough to handle all of life's adult decisions. The thing is, while—thanks to puberty—your body may tell one story, your mind is lagging somewhere between "Mom, I should be able to do whatever I want" and "Every time I make a mistake, I'm expecting a bigger, more experienced adult (my mom) to pick up the pieces." Yes, being a young adult brings forth blatant contradictions, especially when it comes to processing romantic relationships.

For me, because I had seen so many people do marriage the wrong way, I knew a successful one required more than two people who shared the same last name and bed. There had to be money to pay bills, compatibility to get along, and a desire to help one another fulfill their destiny in life. Raging hormones and the best off-camera impression of a couple from a favorite chick flick wasn't going to cut it on even the best day.

That wasn't to say that marriage didn't have some perks that piqued my interest, to put it mildly; however, having a balanced frame of mind was not my strong suit, mostly because so much of my childhood was imbalanced in so many ways, especially socially and emotionally. While I was wise enough to know I was not ready for the responsibilities of marriage, I was so needy for affection—especially from the male gender—that I was willing to put myself in harm's way to partake of marriage's privileges. Patience was a virtue I thought I couldn't afford—and as a result, I paid a high price, but it started way before I lost my virginity (well, gave it away. I know where it went).

On June 17, 1974, despite my mother's troubled pregnancy, my married parents gave birth to a baby girl. My mother told me that because of all of the medication she was on prior to delivering me, for a moment I gave them quite a scare because the doctors feared I had a mental deficiency. After many prayers and a pastor coming in to anoint me (just like the Word says), a miracle took place, and soon I was walking and talking with the best of 'em. To be honest, I don't remember a lot of my early years. I have flashbacks of a sandbox in the backyard of my house in Lincoln, Nebr., memories of Mardi Gras-like beads that hung from an entryway of the house, and two cats affectionately named after the '70s comedy classic, *Laverne and Shirley*. I also vaguely remember that my father was a Dallas Cowboys fan and that I had a surrogate grandmother, whom I am told I visited often, but that's about it. All in all, not too bad—for the moment anyway.

I was two when my parents divorced and my mother moved back to her parents' home in New York. There, things became a little more vivid. I recall a light blue two-story home with an attic and a merry-go-round in the backyard. I remember it was there that I saw the first Christmas tree (that I could recall), had instant Cream O' Wheat for breakfast, and was introduced to such fashionable accessories as my grandfather's golf caps. It was also where I witnessed the love usually reserved for human beings given to my grandmother's poodle, Toy. I recall going to one of the most luxurious apartments I had ever seen, which belonged to my great-grandmother Brown, for one-night slumber parties, pancakes, and *The Brady Bunch*. I also remember going to my great-grandfather and his wife's home where I was spoiled rotten—and was scared to death of their shower curtain with the spider on it. To this day, the memory of it gives me the creeps.

Sure, to be the child of a single mom at age three had its share of dysfunction, but all-in-all, life still seemed to be "a-okay." Then my mother met a man who would become the only father I'd really know for the next twelve years of my life. He was really tall, really dark, and really nice. Soon we developed our own relationship that came with nicknames-n-all. He was my "chocolate cake" and I was his "sweet pie." Looking back, I don't really remember my mother's interaction with him, and the first time I can recall them kissing was at their wedding. My mom had one of those Dorothy Hamill pageboy styles with baby's breath in her hair. She was beautiful, that I know for sure because she always had been. I can't remember what I had on, but I do remember standing at the beginning of an aisle that seemed to go on forever and looking at my tall, soon-to-be-stepfather and his even taller younger brother and thinking to myself, *Something ain't right*, and crying. A lot and loudly.

Looking back, I think that was a huge red flag to everyone in there, especially my mother. You know how they say that a child can see a person's real character? Although I was fifteen before I would fully know what was so wrong with the tall, dark, and nice man whom I first called "chocolate cake," then later, "Daddy," I think deep down inside, on that hot summer day just days before my fourth birthday, I knew something wasn't right with him becoming my mother's husband or my father.

At the time, he was a musician, so we moved to Nashville, Tenn., the home base for his singing group. I was an adult before I knew the financial struggles we had our first few years there. All I recall are roller skates, dolls, and the time I almost lost my life while using an outlet as the ignition for my invisible car. Back then, life still seemed to be pretty good. My mother and I would go downtown at least once a week for story hour at the big, public library, and later we would go window shopping after having lunch at a dainty tea shop. I don't remember much about how my mother and new father interacted with one another, but I do know that was the closest my mother and I would be for quite some time.

I was three weeks shy of six when my baby brother, Jonathan Christian, came onto the scene, and at first, I wasn't very happy about it. It wasn't that I minded having a younger sibling. It was that I minded that younger sibling being a boy. To be honest, the thought of that even being a possibility never even crossed my mind, so when one of my parent's closest friends told me, "Shellie, you have a baby brother," I was less than pleased, and it took some major convincing to get me to go and see him. It was a few years later before I realized just how much of a miracle Jonathan was and would be in my life. He too had a rough time coming into this world, but you wouldn't know it looking at his little face already smiling in the hospital window. That Sabbath in May of 1980 was the day I saw a healthy male image. I would need it.

I'm not sure if things actually got worse for my parents around this time or if I was just old enough to notice some things. At times, it was harder to sleep late at night because they were talking so loudly to one another. This was also the time that I actually remember seeing my mother cry for the first time in my life. There were still good memories, like learning how to ride my bike, stringing popcorn for the Christmas tree, playing outside with the neighborhood kids, receiving pre-Sabbath surprises (like a new purse or dress), and watching my little brother grow up, but as I began elementary school, things definitely got more complicated.

From time to time, the loud, late night talks became

physical altercations, and I didn't know how to handle it. I was too young to keep two adults from hurting one another, but too old to ignore the fact that it was hurting me. So, I would do things to medicate the pain. Sure, they were stupid, but they served as distractions. At first my distractions of choice appeared to be pretty innocent. My mother had always told me I was a very intelligent child, so schoolwork was never much of a challenge for me, although shutting up so that other people could finish their work always was. At first my parents would be called in for my talking. But soon it elevated to talking back to teachers and even a few bouts of shoplifting. My parents would ask me what was going on with me. I didn't know how to say it at the time.

As an adult, I remember my mother sharing stories with me about her childhood. Some of them made me laugh out loud (like the time she fell off of the porch from her tobacco buzz), and some of them made my cry for her on the inside. She came from a home that made our family seem like *The Cosby Show*. Because her father was a Christian ... and an alcoholic, in his drunken state, he would beat my grandmother and his two children, believing he was justified. Sometimes out of frustration, hurt, and rejection, in return my grandmother would beat them as well.

I know my mother loved me, but around my pre-teen years, she too must've been pretty frustrated and felt pretty hurt and rejected. Now, I'm not saying that I wasn't a handful from time to time, but as I got older, there were less girlie dates and more spankings that eight times out of ten started out as my fault, but ended up as beatings (welts and all) that were ten times out of ten her fault. Nothing I did ever seemed good enough for her, and after a while, I stopped trying as hard.

She called it disobedience. I called it getting a tougher skin so the verbal or physical lashings wouldn't hurt so much.

Daddy always took up for me though. That might have been a part of the problem. Although he too was stern, when he spanked me, it never left a bruise or scar. In him I found safety, while in my mother I found fear and resentment; soon he became my favorite parent and my best friend. He seemed to enjoy spending time with me. We listened to music and watched television together and even took long walks. But what I really liked about my Daddy was that I could talk to him about absolutely anything. To him, I was his beautiful princess, and I needed that kind of reassurance. By now, I had big lips and an overbite, acne on my face, and so-so hair—all of the wrong accessories for high school.

Although I knew a lot of people, growing up I only had two lasting childhood friends. One was an angel; the other was my adversary. I met Angela when I was twelve years old, and I envied her from the start. Even in the awkward stages of adolescence, she was what I considered to be perfection—tall, with long hair, great teeth, and flawless skin. She lived with her original parents and four other siblings, and they all seemed to love being with one another on a consistent basis. I went over there every chance I got before she moved away to Atlanta. To this day, she is still one of my closest friends.

Then there was my adversary, Melissa. She too was attractive, but not as beautiful as my distorted self-esteem made her out to be. Since I could remember, she had always been in my life, and to this day, I really don't have one good memory about her. When I was about eight, I remember her locking me out of her house and leaving me with her huge dog. I don't know what left me wetter—his slob or my tears. When I was about ten, she tried to teach me how to write in cursive while sitting in church. All I remember her saying is, "If you weren't so dumb, you would be able to catch on faster." At twelve, while riding in the back seat of her parents' car, I recalled her asking me what I thought my best physical trait was after she ran down the long list of her own. I told her I thought it was my eyes. "Girl, please," she said. "More like your hands." But when you feel like you're not good enough, just enough seems like enough. She wasn't the best kind of friend, but she gave me attention, and I figured bad wasn't worse than none. This mentality got me into a lot of trouble with a lot of people down the pike.

Without my angel, Angela, on my shoulder, Melissa's voice was even louder in high school, which was the last thing I needed. There, I was a minority in every way—including my skin color, but also when it came to my looks, my style of dress, and my personality. And if you want to be popular in high school—back then anyway—being a unique individual rarely works in your favor.

Anyway, at any given time, there were probably literally twelve black girls in the entire school, and because of my "exceptional qualities," I was never the pick of the litter. This is where I began feeling the real effects of being an underdog, and since I had come from a lineage of women who felt hurt and rejected, I found it quite easy to beat up on myself. Often.

Although I had been valedictorian and president of my eighth grade class, after my freshman year, I didn't see anything above a 3.0 (and that was if I was lucky). In high school, although being smart was just as vital as being pretty and popular, guys only paid

you attention if you were a triple threat—and if you
had to be missing one of the three, smart is what they
were willing to lose. I had already received the prize
for academic excellence. I wanted to be rewarded for
social acceptance—especially on the dating scene.

You definitely don't always get what you want. My
first two years consisted of me listening to other girls
talk about the guys they liked versus the ones who
liked them back, and although we never had a prom
(private schools rarely do), we did have a Valentine's
banquet that nearly gave me a heart attack when it
came to finding a date. My first year, my closest male
friend from elementary school served as my escort.
That was the first and last memory of a date that I had
until my senior year, although I did receive some male
attention—more than I asked for or was prepared to
handle—my sophomore year.

One Wednesday before Thanksgiving break, I was
standing outside waiting on my ride home. The two
terrors who I'll call Mutt and Jeff were outside doing
what they always did—teasing girls and touching
them. Throughout my story, I will share different
lessons that different guys have taught me over the
course of my life, and as much as I wish I had skipped
this class, Mutt and Jeff taught me a valuable one: No
one has the right to touch your body or talk to you any
old kind of way at any time, no matter what. But more
than that, we as women—young and old alike—should
value ourselves enough to know that no one has the
right to touch our bodies or talk to us any old kind
of way, no matter what; no matter how starved for
love, attention, admiration, or affection we may be, we
should allow God and our destined mate to fill us.

Although I was a virgin, ironically, I wasn't sexually
ignorant when it came to the basics, just the advanced

courses (like emotional preparation and responsibility). Since I can remember, my mother had age-appropriate books and videos filled with information about sex and why it was something I should wait for until marriage. She was always available for questions, for which she also gave age-appropriate responses. When I about six, I recall watching *Family Feud* with her and the game board "dinging" the answer "make love" to a question I cannot remember. When I turned around and asked her, "Mommy, what's making love?" she said, "It's kissing in the dark, Shell." As I got older, the questions got a little more graphic, while my mother's answers remained age-appropriate. Soon, I was finding myself wanting to know more, and so I enlisted my Daddy as my new sex counselor.

Now, he was great, or so I thought. I later came to see he was not educating me, but rather entertaining himself. No matter what the question, he always had an answer for me, but there are times when you can receive entirely too much information, no matter what the age. For instance, one time he took Melissa and me out to dinner. I couldn't have been more than twelve or so (Melissa was two years older), and we were asking my Daddy questions about guys—you know, what it meant when they did this or said that. Melissa was the connoisseur of male company and served as a greater mouthpiece than I did. At this point, puberty had set in and things were sticking out, and although I had been touched a few times, it was always my breasts, never my heart. I had also been kissed by a pretty popular guy in high school, and in appreciation to the affection I was given, I gave him a card. In response, he gave one back—a torn up version of mine in front of all his friends. My Daddy knew my pain, and so he said something that I guess was supposed to have cheered me up: "If I were to make the perfect woman, she would have your breasts (mine) and your butt (Melissa's)."

I was so starved for attention that at first I smiled, while sticking out my chest like the proudest peacock on the block. A man had told me that I had the makings of the perfect woman. It was a couple of years later before I realized that the man who said it should have never seen me in that way. In the early years, you think that whatever's modeled to you in your home is normal and healthy. When you are trying to get male attention, the first person you run to is your dad—no matter how distorted he may be. A father has the power to set the tone of what goes on outside of the home as well. I mean, if my own dad found me to be sexy, why should I question two horny teens when they sexually assaulted me?

Mutt and Jeff were as different as night and day. One was white, while the other was black. One was an extrovert; the other was an introvert. One was brilliant; the other was … let's just say, less than brilliant. As a matter of fact, if it hadn't have been for the sick bond between them—the beginning stages of sexual addiction due to their own childhood issues and teenage pressures—I don't think they would have even been friends. But their issues made them the best of friends—at least for that semester—and the culprits of what would be one of the most terrifying moments of my life.

Mutt and Jeff were always joking around, and admittedly, I was an extrovert like Mutt (loud, talkative, and a little intimidating), so no one thought anything of it when they pulled me into the back of Jeff's car that day; everyone was laughing, including myself. But as they drove off of the campus, I found myself getting more and more solemn.

"Where are we going?"

"Shut up."

"I want to go back to school."

"Shut up!"

Mutt was in the back seat with me, laughing and rubbing on my breasts with one hand while holding me down with the other. Let me make something clear before I proceed. Those two guys sexually assaulted me that day, no doubt about it, and if I had been older, I would have pressed charges (all the school did when they found out was suspend them for a couple of days), but this was not the first time they had touched a part of my body that was private. In school, whenever they would pinch my butt or pop my bra, I would laugh or giggle in a flirtatious way (so did a lot of the girls). I was so starved for some guy, any guy, to take notice that I never checked them on it. I should have. My need for male attention set the stage for their need to receive sexual stimulation.

As Mutt got louder, so did I. I tried screaming, cursing, and kicking, but they were both athletes and much stronger than I was. When Mutt pulled out a pair of handcuffs, I was horrified, but after a brief wrestling match, they were on my wrists, making me very uncomfortable in every single way. As we reached the back of a strip mall, I grew silent. By this time they had ripped open my shirt as well as my bra and had done about everything they could think of with my breasts. As Mutt reached for the zipper on my pants, I looked at Jeff with glassy eyes. Earlier in the year, I had actually had a mild crush on Jeff, but as most guys had, he rejected me. I was hoping he would again. Being tag teamed in the back of an old car one day before Thanksgiving was not my idea of a romantic first time. People were so used to me being rowdy that I think my silence scared him. After arguing with Mutt for what seemed like an eternity, they let me go and left me there, behind the strip mall—ripped clothes, exposed-n-all.

I went home and eventually told my parents. I guess since I talked about matters of the opposite sex with my father more than my mother at that point, he was better prepared to process the situation. He was furious, but not with me. He was the one I remember going to the school to have a talk with the guys as well as the principal. I was always a little more sexually curious than my mother could handle, so while my Daddy was warning them, my mom was blaming me. "What did you do? What made them comfortable enough to pull you into their car? What were you wearing? You have been known to change your clothes at school from time to time, and it's not like I haven't seen you playing around with the neighborhood kids. Are you telling the truth? It's not like you haven't lied before. I don't know what's wrong with you."

She's right. I had lied before, but not about anything of this magnitude. But her response made me wonder if a part of me deserved it, as if it possibly could have been a consequence of something I had done behind her back or something. Either way, having low self-esteem and topping it off with a bout of sexual assault followed by rejection from your mother only set the stage for more abuse—this time closer to home.

During my high school years, my mother was in a profession that caused her to travel from time to time. By the time I was fifteen, she was actually gone quite a bit, but I didn't mind. Over the course of time, we had gone from being best friends to two people who basically tolerated each other's presence, and at times, we weren't even doing that very well. She made it a point to tell me that she loved me, but I didn't feel like she did, and when you're young, lip service doesn't count for much. I later found out that my mother was hurting in many areas in the worst kind of way, and although she often directed her pain in my direction, it wasn't because she was blaming me. It was that she felt she had nowhere else to go. The only emotionally available person in the house was me, her firstborn, and she often didn't buffer the emotion before soliciting my services. That wasn't an excuse. That was just the fact.

It was many years, prayers, tears, and a conscious reconciliation on both of our parts before I was able to come to that resolve. At the time, all I knew was that she was hurting me, and when she was gone, it stopped, so I wanted her gone as much as possible. Seemingly another man's treasure is one man's junk. On the other hand, my Daddy seemed very bitter about her professional endeavors. Although I've never confirmed this fact with any questions directed his way, I think a part of him resented my mother for becoming who he always wanted to be—a top notch in the entertainment industry, rather than a house-husband. But his anger did not manifest itself in verbal insults or physical altercations. No, he chose a more cryptic route.

I was fifteen, the Christmas that I asked my mother a question that would change our home as I knew it forever. "Do you think Daddy would sexually abuse me?"

I'll never forget the look on her face or the reason that caused me to ask her in the first place. Around age twelve (ironically around the age that I started getting breasts), my Daddy started doing things that I didn't really know were wrong, but I definitely questioned. You already know the butt/breasts incident, but there was more. Things like him allowing me to talk to him while he was in the shower. Things like him exchanging my birth name for "PC" which meant Perfect Curves (I hated that by the way) and singing "Brick House" to me every chance that he got. Things like him initiating explicit sexual conversations even when I preferred to talk on the phone to my friends, or worse yet, go to bed. Things like him never allowing me to lock the bathroom door when my mother was out of town. Things like him sitting on the couch across from me while exposing himself. Things like him touching my breasts. Things like him coming into my room late at night, although to this day, I can't remember why he was there or when he exited.

All of these incidents, coupled with phone calls from strange women and a movie I had seen just a few days before (*Something About Amelia*), led me to this question. I don't really remember what my mother said, but I do recall the look on her face—sheer horror. Finally, we were on the same page emotionally again. At least for a moment.

I wasn't confident in much, but I was certain that my mother would not allow anyone other than herself to harm me in any way. The month that followed that conversation made me more insecure than ever. I had shared with her some of the reasons for my concerns, and yet he was still in the house, in her bed. The two guys at school did not value my body enough to not abuse it, and neither did my Daddy. Now, my mother was sealing the deal.

I later found out that she was in so much shock that she froze up emotionally as well as physically. If there was anyone she thought she needed to protect me from, it definitely wasn't my stepfather—the man I have known and loved since I could remember, the man I found myself preferring over her since I could remember as well. She didn't know what to do. All I knew was she needed to do something, and with every passing day, I found my faith in her ability to shield me from his intentions fading more and more.

One day I came home, and he wasn't there. But the only person who seemed to be relieved about it was me. My mother had lost her husband, and my brother had lost his father. My mother never blamed me for that, but she did interrogate me quite a bit about the details of what had happened. She needed clarity to keep from having a nervous breakdown, but all I saw was a woman who always thought I had a hand in the sexual abuses that were happening to me.

Amazingly, I got through the rest of high school, but it wasn't easy. I was scared, I was wounded, I was angry. But most of all, I was ready to get out of the house to start a new life. There's a real danger in trying to move on into your future without redeeming your past. You look up and find yourself recreating it in some form or fashion over and over … and over again.

chapter two
inside my first love

I had never seen or experienced anything quite like
my freshman year of college. I was so used to being the
awkwardly overlooked minority at my Christian high
school that my transition to a public university with
ten times more blacks—and guys—blew my mind!
Furthermore, to think that even one guy could even
possibly find me attractive sent my heart and hormones
to places I had never been before. Everywhere I
went—from the dorms, to the cafeteria, to class, to
parties—someone was either whistling, flirting, or
blatantly propositioning me for fifteen minutes of my
time, attention, or affection—usually all three.

Although I was curious and had been curious about
sex for quite some time, old habits are hard to break,
and so I did not (immediately) succumb to the thick
fog of sexual pressure that seemed to be clouding the
judgment of most of the girls on campus, including
in my dorm. Actually, although virtually everyone
on my floor was black, after a few conversations and
eaves drops, I came to see that I was still a minority,
this time because I was still a virgin. My first-semester
roommate had a boyfriend who used to sleep over in
our room a couple of nights a week, and my suite mates
were even grander risk takers.

One was a sweet, southern gal who in many ways
seemed a lot like me, except for the raisin-like wrinkles

on her stomach that I had never seen before on any woman. Although in the beginning she wouldn't tell me where they came from, even when I asked, one day without warning I opened the door (as was customary with us) to borrow one of her curling irons and found her sitting on the bed crying with pictures of a little girl spread out over her sheets. I assumed it was her baby sister. She told me it was her baby daughter. She had given up her child for adoption before she came to school.

Her roommate—my other suite mate—was the first mulatto female I could recall actually being friends with, as well as the first girl my age who I had ever seen grinding on guys at parties, getting drunk after them, or admitting to not only having sex on a pretty regular basis, but often initiating it. She had long hair and flawless skin, and although I was pretty outgoing, I was still somewhat naïve; she had a boldness that made me more nervous and envious than comfortable. I think she knew it, because she often went into graphic details about what she had done with guys in the past and what she was willing to do, at the right time, for the right one, even if he wasn't her husband. She often left me speechless—and that's a major accomplishment.

There were some similarities to high school though, such as the fact that soon, seemingly everyone had a boyfriend or a "homey-lover-friend," which is known to some as a "friend with benefits," except for me. Once again I stood out and didn't fit in, but this time for slightly different reasons. While people still never understood my fashion sense (I actually won an award for being what they considered tacky my freshman year), at a major university, there were bigger fish to fry. For one, I was very outgoing, so I had no problem approaching people I didn't know to spark up a conversation. On the social scene, I persevered, and in no time, I was pretty well known around campus—not because I was perceived as pretty or promiscuous, but because I was not much of either, and yet was cool enough to hook guys up with my pretty and promiscuous friends.

Even the girls found me odd, but not much of a competitor, so they had the tendency to share a lot with me—their past, their secrets, their food, their clothes. When it came to going to parties, I was often the designated driver, and when it came to sneaking their boyfriends in and out of our dorm, I was often the one placed on door duty. However, when it came to having my own boyfriend, I was still the loner, and although in high school I was pretty used to that, back then I had convinced myself that it wasn't that no one wanted me, it was just that the pickings were slim. I now had to find another lie to tell myself. That one was no longer the truth by a long shot.

The first semester, no boyfriend, or homey-lover-friend, entered my heart or dorm room, but I did meet two guys—two guys who would never become my boyfriends, but still would fill some of the void for years to come. I came to know Austin and Anthony under the most interesting circumstances. Remember, I was someone who had no trouble approaching strangers, so one day in the cafeteria, I walked up to the table and said hello. Actually, I had met Austin once before, so I felt I had a point of reference. Guess not, because as I helped myself to a seat, the first greeting I received was from Anthony—although it wasn't really directed at me.

"Who the h--- is this?"

The response startled me, but his bold nonchalance

intrigued me as well. He was offensive and outspoken—two things I also had the tendency to be at times.

"This is … what's your name, again? Shellie, right?"

That was Austin—the other side of my personality. He was intelligent, charismatic—not strikingly attractive, but cute enough to make you want to know more about him.

"That's right!"

From that point on, I can't remember a time when those two were not in my life. As a matter of fact, many referred to us as the Three Musketeers. I remember watching movies in their rooms, having lunch with them in the student center, and talking to at least one of them on the phone at least once a day. They were my male buddies, and I was grateful for them (time would tell just how much in chapters to come). But, I had enough friends. I wanted what every girl on the yard seemed to have—or at least what every guy wanted—a companion. As close as I had gotten to my suite mates and my two male sidekicks, there were times when none of them were available because they all were with someone else … of the opposite sex … for the night. Nights alone were pretty cold, so I used those times to dream of a guy of my very own. Be careful what you wish for.

Despite all of the sexual things that had already happened to me before I even set foot on campus, looking back, I know God was trying to protect me from the pain of promiscuity. He even went so far as to have my first on-campus male experience be with a guy who had no intentions of sleeping with me. Marcus was shy, sweet, and beyond fine. A lot of girls wanted him, and he could have had the cream of the crop, but he didn't oblige. To me, that made him even more stunning. Whenever I saw him coming from or going to class, my heart would skip a couple of beats. Trust me when I say that he was just that fine—so much so that he was featured in a sorority calendar that premiered just a semester before, and his picture continued to be on the minds and lips of women across campus. One day, I was sitting on the steps of the student center with a friend of his as he was passing by.

"Does he have a girlfriend?"

"Does it matter?" His friend immediately responded. I didn't really know how to answer that. In high school it did. In college, having a girlfriend seemed to be code for "speak to me at night, not in the day, so that my girl won't find out about us."

"I'll hook you up."

And he did. For the rest of the semester and the first month of the second semester, Marcus and I spent a lot of time together—so much so that some of the guys in the dorm used to tease me about being a tenant. I liked him, and we enjoyed each other's company—there was an intimacy, but there was never sex involved. As a matter of fact, I can count on one hand how many times we even kissed. The physical intimacy pretty much stopped there. I'm not sure why. Maybe he found my personality attractive, but not my physical being. Maybe he was one of the few guys who was faithful to his girl in the day and in the night (she was in school some miles away). Or maybe God was trying to spare me from what was to come. I don't think I ever told Marcus thank you for not taking advantage of the priceless gift I didn't value at the time, and so if you're reading this and recognize yourself in my story, "Thanks." However, there was a catch.

Remember when I said that each male in my life

has taught me a valuable lesson? Marcus wasn't exempt. Although we didn't cross the line, there were times we definitely pushed it, because Marcus had a girlfriend. I may not have given him my virginity, but our relationship definitely gave me the impression that dating other people's men didn't really matter. It was years and years before I thought otherwise.

However, Marcus was not the guy to whom I was referring when I said I should've been more careful about what I wished for. Come to think of it, of all the "relationships" I had in college, he was probably the least dramatic. If Marcus was a slight drizzle, David was a typhoon.

One of the girls I had come to befriend my freshman year was the pretty and promiscuous kind to whom I was referring; guys definitely had her on their radar. When walking together, we rarely got to class on time, because every guy we saw would stop her for some one-minute game. I'm not sure what drew me to Dee Dee. Yes, I do. Dee Dee was drawn to me. Although I was cool with a few of the girls around campus, for the most part when it came to befriending them, the energy was pretty competitive simply because I was female; when it came to me and Dee Dee, I was probably doing her a favor, because for every one guy who approached me, there were ten who wanted her.

In no time, we had become so close that I often found myself spending the night in her dorm room, and she often spent the night at my mother's house on the weekends. She shared stories with me about her tumultuous relationship with her parents, and I did the same. The closer we got, the more we seemed to have in common. We were both really intelligent and funny and grew up in church. But there were also differences. While Dee Dee was away at school, her mother took care of her daughter. And when Dee Dee hurt, she would use sex, weed, and alcohol to ease the pain. I would use the need for other people's attention to medicate mine—even if that meant skipping class to go to the mall, doing other people's homework, or being around the increasing number of "Dee Dees" on campus—the ones who also used sex, weed, and alcohol to medicate their pain.

Thankfully, I was never really interested in what the weed and alcohol had to offer, but that sex thing was captivating me more and more. Seemingly everybody was doing it, so there must've been something to it, right? When it came to sex, I had been the odd woman out for way too long, and I decided it was high time I focused on fitting in.

"I have someone I want you to meet," Dee Dee said two weeks before Valentine's Day. Actually she had been saying it for a couple of months now, but the thought of being without someone on February 14 again was enough to pique my interest this time.

"Who is it?" I sighed. I tried to act like I didn't care, but I did.

"His name is David. He's one of my boyfriend's friends."

I had already met Dee Dee's boyfriend, and if what they said about birds flocking together was true, then I wasn't going to be impressed. Sure he looked all right, but Samson was not the most intelligent or articulate cat. He seemed nice enough though. He was always buying Dee Dee things, and if we all went out, he would pick up the whole tab. But Samson had another side to him. It was rare that he and Dee Dee could spend twelve hours together without one of them hitting the other. Plus he had a record for shooting some guy his sister used to date. He definitely was not my idea of marriage or dating material. Still, a Valentine couldn't hurt. Don't be so sure.

"... He's coming up for the game, tomorrow. Come by the room and meet him, okay?"

If I said I wasn't nervous about my first and only blind date, I'd be lying. I spent that entire evening and the next day trying to figure out what I was going to wear, how I was going to do my hair, and what would be my plan of escape should he not be my type. I took a deep breath as I knocked lightly on the door and entered Dee Dee's room. Actually, there were a few guys in there, so I wasn't sure which one was "the one," but if it was the first guy I saw after Samson, I was prepared to make an immediate about-face.

"Shellie, this is David."

I held my breath as I followed her index finger. It was a tall, dark guy with an athletic build in the back of the room. He had wavy hair, nice lips, and slanted, almond eyes. Now that was more like it.

It goes without saying that David was my Valentine that year. I remember he got me a card, a balloon, and a rose—my first gift from a guy ... ever. It was months later before I knew that Dee Dee had actually bought the card and signed it. Geesh.

For weeks we were inseparable. During the week, he would take the hour-plus ride to my school with Samson, and on the weekends, I would take the hour-plus ride with them to their hometown. We would find ourselves talking for hours on the phone about everything from our families to our views on politics, education, and spirituality. And although in months to come I would discover just how much alike he and Samson were, if there was one thing that set them apart, it was David's intelligence. He was darn near brilliant, which outshined the long list of flaws and red

flags God was trying to show me about him before it
was too late.

While we were in the relationship, it seemed that
it was years before we had sex for the first time, but
when I really think about it, it was probably only eight
weeks from the time we first met. The first six weeks
were spent kissing, fondling, and with me saying "no."
The last two weeks were spent kissing, fondling, and
David asking me if I was sure. If there is anything
about which I can warn a rookie in the game of lust,
it's that, like the serpent in the Garden of Eden,
someone who wants to sleep with you will be patient.
They will converse and if necessary, charm you long
enough that you begin to believe that having sex with
them is the right thing to do even if it's under the
wrong circumstances.

My first time was in his mother's bed in his mother's
house while we were supposed to be babysitting his
little sister, who lay asleep in another room. It was a
mediocre experience in the sense that it was not as
painful or as grand as some of my friends tried to make
it sound. It was awkward, it was relatively quick, and
it was not what I thought it was going to be, although
I must say that David tried to make it as special as he
could—in his mother's house, in her bed, with his sister
sleeping in the other room. The reality is, dreamy sex
is meant for a committed couple—the ones who have
rings on the third fingers of their left hands to prove it.

For the next several weeks, David and I tried hard
at making sex easier. He would kiss me a lot before
and hold me a lot after, but the during part remained
to be something that just couldn't be mastered. I could
tell that it was starting to embarrass him, and so while
I was skipping class to see him, I took up Faking It
101 on my downtime. Soon, I became a star pupil. The

more time I spent on his turf, the more I had come to know that while he may have been my first, I was much farther down his hit list. I didn't want to lose him, so I did whatever I had to do to keep him—both in and out of bed.

The first lesson from David: Never give so much of yourself to someone that you lose yourself—especially if you were just holding on to fragments of you in the first place. With that said, I believe that there's a certain loyalty that every woman has when it comes to her first sexual experience. I also believe that God put it there—except it was designed only for your husband and not your first boyfriend. Believe me when I say that when it came to my devotion to David, Jay-Z and Beyoncé's video had nothin' on us. We were the modern-day Bonnie and Clyde on a whole 'nother level. As I became more familiar with David and his world, he became comfortable with exposing me to more of it.

It soon became more and more apparent that the domestic disputes between Dee Dee and Samson were the way most young couples "showed their love for one another" in that small town, and that weed and alcohol were consumed just as much, if not more, than sweet tea on summer afternoons or biscuits-n-gravy on Sunday mornings. Once again I found myself in a place where I didn't really fit in, but at this point, I had gotten so used to doing whatever I had to do to make David and myself work that I began to confuse compromises with sacrifices. Many times I found myself silently watching my girlfriend Dee Dee catch a beat down by her boyfriend—even once in her grandparent's house while her grandparents were in another room. I continuously let David borrow my car to "make runs," even when I didn't know where he was going, and even though he never returned when he said he would or with the car in the condition it was in when he took it (he never replaced the gas, and one time it had a dent in it). I ignored his spiraled digression from cigarettes to weed and then from smoking weed to selling it. I even stayed with him after I was arrested and placed in a holding cell one night for the gun that was found under my car seat (my record was dropped, but that began a series of arrests for him and his group of so-called friends). I gave up school (although I was still enrolled, I rarely went to class); my weekends (after a while, his desire to spend time with me really meant time with my car); my boundaries (he could basically talk me into or out of anything he wanted); and soon even my sanity—all in the name of love, or what I thought was love at the time. Even then, God would bring I Corinthians 13—the scriptures I had to memorize in elementary school—to my remembrance. The first word used to describe love was patient. But anything David wanted from me, even if it was more than I could afford to give, I gave.

He said it couldn't wait.

chapter three
inside my first pregnancy

I'll never forget the first time I saw a positive sign on a pregnancy test. David and I had been sexually involved for several months now, and for the most part, everything was going well. Well, kind of.

Actually, it was during this time that I was seeing more and more things about him and his lifestyle that should have sent me running for the hills rather than his arms. By now, he was a full-fledged drug dealer, which meant he only went to school part-time. He was still calling me every day and telling me that he loved me, but the frequency was getting to be less, and the high-pitched voices I overheard in the background were becoming more. Because he was making more of his own money—and lots of it, there was less of a need for mine, so we didn't see each other as much, although he would make stops by my house at least once a week while either heading to or coming from a drop off. Soon his fast-paced way of life caught up to him, and he got arrested. As a matter of fact, David was in a group home when I received the news in the form of a pink plus sign.

I sat on the toilet for what seemed like forever talking to myself. "Pregnant. I'm pregnant? What the heck am I going to do?" My mother didn't even know I was having sex, and she definitely didn't know it was with David. The only encounters she had with him was in passing the phone to me after saying, "Shellie, you need to teach your friends how to speak when they call over here. 'Can I speak to Shellie?' or 'Is Shellie there?' isn't good enough."

I'm sure if she knew what I knew on that 4th of July, she would have preferred his rudeness to my newfound news any day. For a moment, I sat there in awe, thinking: *I am pregnant. I am carrying the man I love's child. It's really true that when you miss your period, you should take a test.*

Then I sat in fear feeling: *I am still in school. I don't have any money. This will just confirm the insulting things my mother said to me even when I was a virgin. I am going to have to face my friends, my school, and my church. My baby's father is a drug dealer. I'm really pregnant. Oh God, I'm really pregnant.*

I decided I would keep all of this information to myself—for now. I knew enough about pregnancy from girls at school to know that there wasn't too much I could do about it anyway until I was farther along. I had made plans with some of my friends to attend an Independence Day party, and so I got dressed and went.

As much as I tried to ignore it, the words "I'm pregnant" consumed my every thought, my every breath—so much so that when my friend Christopher answered the door, greeted me, and asked how I was, the first thing that came out of my mouth in a low whisper was, "I'm pregnant." He must've thought that the loud noises behind him prevented him from hearing me right.

"I'm sorry. You're what?"

After confirming that what he first heard was true, he stood there in the same awe that I had been in just a few minutes before. Christopher was four years older

than I was and a victim of one of my crushes not too
many years before. But because he always saw me as
a little sister and a virgin, nothing ever came of it. We
hadn't spoken in a while, so I'm sure he still thought of
me in that way, which is why I'm sure he was in shock.

"Oh my God, Shellie. Do you need anything? Do
you want some water or a seat to sit down?"

What I wanted was to not be pregnant, but I
accepted his offer for a chair and a drink and sat
quietly as I watched the party move before me. How
long was I going to wait before telling my thug-for-a-
man boyfriend that I was carrying his child? That was
the first obstacle I had to cross. It was harder than I
expected, but not for the reasons I had predicted.

"Pregnant? You, pregnant?" Those were the first
fragmented sentences I recall coming out of his mouth.
"You, carrying my baby?" soon followed. But unlike
me, his tone was not of shock or stress. He actually
seemed happy about it. For the next few weeks, we
talked about my condition and shared our opinions on
how it should be handled. For David, abortion was
never a consideration, let alone an option.

"How you gonna say you love me and want to kill my
child?"

That was a pretty loaded question, and I didn't have
any answers. I only retorted with more questions.

"How are you gonna raise our child locked up or
selling drugs?"

He too didn't have any immediate resolves. All
he knew was that the fatherless son now had the
opportunity to raise his own baby—to fix all of the
things that had gone wrong in his relationship with his
dad. All I knew was that my mind and my body were
not interested in serving as anyone's therapy.

I decided to call Melissa and ask her what to do.

Looking back, I don't know what I was thinking. She
never steered me into the right direction before, but
as they say, misery loves company, and I knew that if
anyone was well-versed on the subject of unplanned
pregnancies, it would be her. She immediately referred
me to the place she had went to abort more than one of
her own children.

"Girl, they don't have any picketers and no one
will know your business. Some people go to get birth
control pills, some people go for AIDS tests, and others
go just to see a gynecologist, so the only way people
will know is if you tell 'em. On top of that, they offer
twilight sleep; you can ask to be put to sleep, and you
won't feel a thing."

And you won't feel a thing. Those few words came to
haunt me later in life.

I wasn't sure what I was going to do at that point.
My boyfriend wanted me to keep it, and I didn't know
what I wanted. I knew that abortion was wrong, a
sin, but God and I weren't the closest at the time, and
so He was not on the top of my priority list. I tried
to envision what my life would be like with a little
person in it, and everything seemed so foggy. In so
many ways, I still felt like a child myself, in need of
her mother's love and approval, and I didn't know if a
needy person had anything to give—even if it's their
own flesh and blood.

If there was one thing God and David had in
common at the time, it was that neither of them
approved of the ultimate decision to terminate my
pregnancy, but I concluded that it was best for me.
Who's to say whether either one of them would have
stuck it out with me for the long haul if I had kept
the child? And that was a bet I wasn't willing to lose.
Because David was in a group home and not juvenile,

he could have gotten a pass to go with me, but his adamant disapproval required that I find someone else to escort me, per the clinic's recommendation. The last words I remember David saying were, "If you really loved me, you wouldn't kill our child." After all that we had been through, that was the first time I ever questioned my loyalty to him and our relationship.

A high school girlfriend of mine took me instead. Sadly enough, she had recently experienced her own termination from a guy who had her and his girlfriend pregnant at the same time. She said he didn't even have the decency to go with her (although he did pay for it), so she had to go alone. She never wanted anyone to have to experience that.

I sat in the clinic for what seemed like hours. First, they had me take another test just to be sure. Then, they had me meet with the financial department to make my payment ($365 at the time). After thirty minutes or so, a nurse called my name so they could weigh me, take my blood pressure, and remove my finger nail polish (a requirement so they can check your blood pressure during the procedure). But of all the strangers I had met during such a personal time, perhaps who stood out more than anyone was the nurse who took my blood. She had on the radio, was singing, and seemed really upbeat to be prepping me for such a morbid procedure.

"Awh, what's up girl? Be still now, so I can hook you up."

She was so animated, that for a moment, I forgot that I was walking in the valley of the shadow of death. After she finished, she said something that made me remember.

"I'll probably see you next year. Eighty percent of all women return within a year."

Was that true? And more importantly, was she on something? There was no way I would be putting myself through the mental or physical stress, emotional trauma, or financial sacrifice that it took to come to this decision. She can forget that.

Remember I said this. It will come in handy later.

I was then taken into a room to speak with a so-called counselor. She reviewed with me everything that was about to take place, and asked me if I had any questions. Half of the things she pointed to on the diagram I didn't even know were inside of my body, and so I had plenty of questions, but I was internally silenced when she went into her song and dance about how proud they all were to be able to provide me with this option.

"It is no one's choice but the woman, and if she is not ready to become a mother, we are glad to be able to assist her in her decision."

C'mon. Even I knew that in the grand scheme of things, it wasn't my choice, and it definitely wasn't something I was proud of, but I guess after a while, that's what she had to tell herself to keep from going insane. I knew for the past week or so, I had been filling my mind up with some ridiculous untruths for the exact same reasons. Ones like, "It won't be so bad," "It will be over before you know it," "I can handle this on my own," and "I am through having sex … but if I do fall, I will always use protection."

After her ten-minute consultation, I was taken into a room with a monitor. The nurse told me to take off my clothes, put on a gown, and lie on my back. A few moments later, she came in and turned the monitor away from my face. She squirted some cold jelly-like ointment on my stomach and moved it around until I heard a clicking sound. She then made a print out, turned off the monitor, and walked out. In elementary school, I had a friend whose mother did that for a living, so I knew what the nurse was after. She was looking for my baby so they could take it away. A sick irony, I know.

Soon, I was led into an all white room with a tray of steel instruments beside the table I was told to get up on. I was then instructed to lie down once more and spread my legs. A nurse was at my side tying a syringe around my arm. "This is going to sting just a little bit," she said.

"What is it?" I asked, surprised I could still speak.

"It is anesthesia to put you to sleep."

"Are you sure it's going to work? I'm a little scared."

"Don't be. Just take a deep breath and count from one to ten backwards."

I looked toward my thighs, but my gown was in the way; I felt a warm metal instrument go inside of me — something very similar to what I experienced when I had my first pap smear. I looked to the left and saw a clear, glass jar, and suddenly I felt like the walls were caving in.

"I'm scared. How will I know if I ..."

My next memory was opening my eyes and feeling slightly nauseated. There were other women around me, and I had my clothes back on. Where was I? What the heck was going on? I was too weak to speak and too disoriented to move, so I waited until a nurse came to me and asked if I would like some soda or crackers. My mouth was dry, so I nodded my head "yes."

"Now, I have placed a packet right here on your seat," she said. "It has your prescriptions in it. One is for pain, one is to shrink your uterus back to size, and the other is for birth control pills." Everything else trailed off at that point. Here I was, just hours from recovering from a pregnancy, and she was talking about how to prevent the next one.

"Your friend is waiting for you outside. We will help you to the door in about ten more minutes."

I don't recall saying anything to my girlfriend on the ride home, but I do remember getting a call from Melissa later that evening. She was checking in to see how everything had gone and if her referral had been a good one. David didn't call me that night or for several nights to follow. That's okay. I wasn't really speaking to myself either.

chapter four
inside my first lust and...

In many ways, that was the beginning of the end for me and David. We had been so used to being in one another's lives that I think we confused love for habit, so we tried to stick it out, but the respect was already gone. His thug-lifestyle was becoming progressively worse. Soon he was not only selling and smoking weed, but cocaine as well. Although he never displayed violence toward me, his bad temper was becoming less and less sporadic, which led to more fights on the streets and even more arrests. His "I love yous" were soon replaced with "I'll call you later," and although we were still sexually active (that's right, I was still having sex), it had the tendency to take place when he was intoxicated and with little regard to my satisfaction. I had even gotten into a very heated verbal altercation with his mother after she covered up a cheating incident between him and a white girl I had never seen before. Now she and I were enemies. Not the girl. His mother.

Many years later, David shared with me that my abortion sent him into a deep depression, even if he didn't know it at the beginning. He didn't feel very loved by his parents, he felt very used by his friends, and the one person he thought he could depend on, the one he thought would love him and everything about him unconditionally was me. Yet, I didn't even want to carry his child. For him and his self-worth, that was the last straw.

Because he had been the only man I had ever loved, I didn't know quite how to end it, so I didn't, but it definitely tapered off, and things definitely got worse. He didn't call me as much and came to see me even less, so I set my sights on someone else to help me heal the wounds. I should've taken the time to deal with my breakup, as well as the loss of my firstborn child, but those were realities I was not yet ready to face. Like the seasons, my first love was fading out of my life, while my first lust was coming in.

Michael was an Adonis, and everyone knew it. He was an ex-basketball player, a grad student, and the life of the party — no matter what the occasion. Michael was well-versed in all kinds of music (he introduced me to Lenny Kravitz) and well-adapted to all environments and women. One day you may see him with the prim and proper, the next with the "bout it, bout it" crowd, but no matter what, it was rare that you would not see him in the presence of a lady.

Our chance meetings took place in the campus student center, and they were always brief. He would comment on my clothes, I would comment on his style overall, but nothing was really exchanged beyond courtesies. It didn't matter, though. I soon found myself living for those two-liner exchanges every other day, and like a potential drug addict after his first hit, soon I found myself wanting more.

As "luck" would have it, not long after, I befriended his roommate Jim, and it wasn't long before I had finagled my way into an invitation to his home for a barbecue. That was when Michael and I got better acquainted, and we soon figured out that we had more than quick wit in common. We began talking on the phone at first for brief moments, but then for hours discussing everything from music and religion to men and women. Michael had a girlfriend, but it was hard for me to take the relationship seriously, let alone respect it or care, because most of the time we were talking about any other woman but her. It was not rare for him to ask me to hook him up with someone he saw me with or to ask for the low-down on one of the girls in my dorm. To me this so-called girlfriend was "out of sight, out of mind." I was feelin' this brother, and because it was the first guy I had really liked since David, I blindly followed by heart ... or rather, my hormones.

Amazingly, sex was never a big topic of conversation for us. He knew that I was getting over my ex and that he had been my first. I knew that he didn't have an ex and that his girlfriend was nowhere close to being his first, but that was about the extent of it. I think that was what made me want to know more about him. I was so used to guys being overtly and immaturely blatant when it came to the subject matter that Michael was a welcome change—and a challenge. Without knowing it or planning it, we found ourselves becoming good friends. I wanted more and didn't know how to get it, but that was good enough.

Then one day, I was walking from one dorm to another when he passed me in his car. He honked his horn and asked me to get in, and I did. We had become cool, so that wasn't really strange—however, what followed was.

"Show me your breasts."

Michael seemingly lived for the element of surprise, so initially I thought nothing of it.

"Whatever, boy."

"I'm serious. Show me your breasts."

I sat there stunned. Was he coming on to me, Shellie? Here I was, just inches away from the only man who replaced David in all of my fantasies, and here he was propositioning me? It was unreal.

"Right here? Right now?" I said barely above a whisper.

"Sure. No one can see us."

If anyone would have told me that I would be flashing some guy who wasn't even my boyfriend in a car by choice (remember, I had been exposed in a car once before), I would have told them that they didn't know me at all. But I did it, so maybe I didn't know myself. As with most risky things in life, our intimate encounters became more frequent and more risqué. Michael was the first person with whom I had experienced oral sex (something my boyfriend thought was too disgusting), and because I had never had an orgasm before, the feeling that gave me sent me to a whole 'nother level of stupefied devotion. I was strung out in a major, major way.

I'm sure it goes without saying that in no time, I had encountered my second sex partner (as it relates to intercourse), and although I figured that different partners would bring about different experiences, I didn't know just how distinctive until I had gotten more deeply involved. On one hand, it wasn't nearly as often that I had to act like I was physically satisfied with Michael, but on the other hand, whenever David and I would sleep together, it would be just that—he would stay the whole night and hold me for as long as I desired. Michael, on the other hand, would turn me over, do his business, and then leave the room to watch a game on television. There was never any holding or hugging, and now that I think about it, rarely any kissing.

There were times when he would do something special like create a theme room with neon lights and music, but looking back, that was probably more for him than for me—perhaps to keep from being bored. And what about the condoms? We started out using them, but then he said that he didn't want to, and since he knew I had only been with one person, he felt I was safe so long as I stayed honest with him about the cycle of my period (I never did fill that prescription for birth control). Here he was cheating on his girlfriend, and I was only concerned with what he thought about my sexual history.

For several months, we maintained this "down low" affair. There were even a couple of times when his girlfriend was at the house when I was there, but I always knew how to play the "friend" role. But as they say, all seemingly good things must come to an end. In hindsight, the more appropriate saying would have to be, all bad things get worse.

One weekend while my mother was out of town, I borrowed her car, and, without her knowing my secret lifestyle, it was almost eerie what she said. "Shellie, don't take my car up and down the highway all weekend. It needs new tires, and I can't afford to get them until I get back."

As soon as those keys were placed into my hand, I immediately erased all that she had said from my mind. I dropped her off at the airport and headed to Michael's house, some twenty miles away. About five miles from the exit, I found myself in a rain shower with a car slamming on his brakes just a few hundred feet ahead of me.

"No problem. I'll slam on my brakes too," I thought. Only when I attempted to use mine, nothing happened. For a brief moment, I saw my life flash before my eyes as I turned my steering wheel to the right, opting for the grass, rather than the car before me. By the grace of God, my car stopped just in front of a tree, but by my carnal rebellion did not give me time to reflect on the fact that God was trying to tell me the same thing that my mother did—go home; stay off the roads and out of trouble. Instead, I'm ashamed to say that I had the audacity to say, "Thank you, Lord," and then continued on my journey to Michael's house and the last time we would ever sleep together. To this day, I wonder if God was trying to spare me from more than fornication with the accident I almost experienced.

If anyone has ever told you that sex won't change a friendship, they lied. It's amazing how the very thing that's meant to be a gift for married folks can be a curse for singles. The more Michael and I were physically intimate, the less we had to talk about, and soon things became very tense. I believe he was experiencing guilt mixed with fear when it came to cheating on his girlfriend, and I found myself missing being held and told that I was loved. No matter how fine Michael was or how he made me feel on a physical level, it couldn't compare to my emotional bond to David—a very wise lesson we can all learn when it comes to having sex purely for physical reasons.

Although the conversations with David were not as consistent as they once had been, they still were happening. I took advantage of his "check ins" and began letting him know how I was feeling, saying that I missed him, when in reality, I was probably more desperate for affection than anything else. He must've had needs too, because on my birthday (June), rather than giving me a card or a cake, he gave me sex—and then a really big fight that led me to wonder just what I missed in the first place.

Old habits die hard. I had never used a condom with David, and I didn't then. So now, here I was, sexually involved with two men and unprotected with both of them. My period came at the end of the month, so I thought I was home free ... until the end of July, when no menstrual cycle arrived.

Another pregnancy test later—this time one that showed two blue lines instead of one—I was in a worse predicament than ever. Not only did I not have a boyfriend as I had before, but there were two potential fathers, and because I had slept with them so closely together, I wasn't one-hundred percent sure of who the father was—something you couldn't have paid me to think would be my reality ... ever. I had gotten pretty used to the rhythm method and counting my days, and when you think about it, almost a year and a half of unprotected sex on a regular basis without protection and resulting in only two pregnancies wasn't super ridiculous odds. Therefore, I was betting that it was David's child and not Michael's, but I decided to tell them both just to be sure.

The first person I told was Michael. After all, although he was my "friend with benefits," he was my friend. When I called him, he said, "Gee Shell, that's too bad. I gotta go. I'll call you later." Of course he never did. And when I tried calling him, his roommate would always say he wasn't there or that he would return my call.

When I told David, because of how he responded to my first pregnancy, I figured he would look at this as a time of redemption. Instead he told me that he didn't want me to have it, and that he would pay for my abortion. With the fact that I still had not shared with my family that I was now what was considered promiscuous, and since neither man was showing any level of support, I figured that abortion was my best and only option. I called David to redeem the money that he promised, and he hung up in my face and then blocked my calls. This was the man who claimed to love me, even if we were broken up, and suddenly he was treating me like some two-cent whore. What was I going to do?

I shared my dilemma with a couple of my girlfriends, and they all agreed that an abortion would be the best resolution, so they donated money to my emergency fund. This time, one of the purest-spirited women I have ever known went with me to the same clinic for the same reason that I went just thirteen months before — not because she agreed with my decision, not because she thought it was the only way out, but because she loved me so much that she didn't want me to be alone. The nurse who took my blood the first time must've been prophetic. She told me I would return in July, and I did in August.

Those months to follow were some of the most difficult in my life. I was now a woman who had two abortions before she was even twenty-one, all the while trying to hide the fact that I was sexually active from my mother for fear that it would make our relationship even more tumultuous. I had flunked out of school because of my poor grades, and so I had to move back home. I was no longer friends with Michael, and to top it all off, word had gotten to me that David was expecting the birth of his daughter in just a few months (which explains why he was so distant when I shared with him my news of being pregnant. He would've had two babies just a few months apart). But more than anything, what I was still trying to put my mind around was the fact that when I woke up from my second stint of anesthesia and steel, I asked the nurse

just how far I was, and rather than being the six to
eight weeks that I expected, I was told that I was a
whopping thirteen weeks, which meant that there was
a greater chance Michael had been the father, and that
following my period was not a surefire way of knowing
whether or not I was pregnant—something my mother
had told me years before because she had a cycle for a
few months while being pregnant with me.

The icing on this cake of chaos was one October
night, just two months after I suffered the loss of my
second child—alone—I received a long distance phone
call from Michael. He was overseas playing basketball,
and he had called to say—no, warn—no, *threaten* me—
to never tell his girlfriend that I had been pregnant.
No "how are you?" No "I know I was a jerk for never
checking in to make sure you were all right." No "do
you need anything?" For the first time since he had
come into my life, I saw that everything about us, even
my sexual satisfaction, was about him. He didn't care
about my feelings or the fate of the unborn child, just
his comfort level. His blatant selfishness stabbed me to
the very core, but I kept my cool. I assured him that
things would be fine. And then I began plotting out my
revenge.

chapter five
inside my loss

Although I was what society would consider to be a sexual late bloomer, I was definitely making up for lost time. In the course of two years, I had lost my virginity, two of my children, and what little dignity I had left. Because of this sad fact, I was willing to do more than I should have to get a man to like me, but I had still not stooped so low as to do whatever they wanted when they didn't like me anymore. No, not yet.

So, when Michael arrived back into town from playing overseas, I had a nice little reunion waiting for him. By this time, I had seen it all at school: a guy who was shot by a another guy at a party—over a girl; a girl who hit another girl over the head with a beer bottle— over a guy; girls who made it their mission to take other women's men and men who made it their mission to seek out those kinds of women. Because Michael was an expert when it came to enticing members of the opposite sex, I didn't want to be obvious with my plan. I was bitter. So bitter that I was determined he was going to feel as pained, scarred, intimidated, and fed up as I had the day I had my second abortion and the night I received his international phone call.

Over the past several months, I befriended his girlfriend, even though I really didn't like her very much. But this wasn't about liking her. It was about hating him. Soon hanging out at her house became the norm, so she was more than comfortable with me sitting on her living room floor when Michael walked into her apartment one hot summer day. Today, I am proud to say that I have gotten over everything as it relates to my situation with Michael; but that's now. This was then. And then I would have loved to have a Polaroid shot of the look on his face when he saw me for the first time in his girlfriend's house acting more like her sister than his enemy. Word to the wise, fellas: Bitter women are like Gremlins; they don't die, they multiply.

Anyway, I didn't do anything immediately. I spent the next couple of weeks basking in the glow and glory of my power to make him feel uncomfortable. Then one day, while his girlfriend and I were alone, I pulled off a stellar performance. My freshman year, I had taken a beginner's acting class in which the teacher instructed us to remember something devastating in our past in order to show deep present tense emotion for any given scenario. I had a lot of memories to choose from, and in no time, the tears were flowing.

"Shellie, what is it? What's wrong?" she asked, kneeling beside me.

"I'm just having a rough day. I don't want to talk about it," I said.

"C'mon. I've never seen you cry like this. You can tell me."

And with her permission, I did. I told her everything. I told her about my affair with her man. I told her about the times when she had approached his back door while I was exiting his bedroom door. I told her about the pregnancy and termination that he did not participate in on any level, and I told her about the October night phone call when he asked me not to tell her about everything I had just said to her.

He had thrown me out on my heart. She threw him out on his butt; now neither one of us had a dwelling place. But I didn't care about him. It was every self-centered person for himself at this point. I had been wounded on lust's battlefield, and I was tired of being the only casualty.

Gratefully, this was when Damien came onto the scene. He's the only guy in my story whose name has not been changed to protect his identity, mostly because his character doesn't need it. I can confidently say that if my brother was the first healthy male image to change my life, Damien was my second.

Damien and I met our freshman year, but we didn't hit it off right off the bat. Sure, he was cool enough, but initially it didn't seem like we had a lot in common. This may have been because my girlfriend, Alicia, had a major crush on him, so I never tried to get to know him beyond inquiring why he didn't like her as much as she seemed to like him. However, I did get along pretty well with his roommate, Shane, and as we got closer, my interaction with Damien became more consistent. Still, I didn't think too much of it at the time. I was still licking the wounds from my past two fiascoes, and besides the fact that my girl had her sights set on him, on the physical level, Damien just wasn't my type. So, after returning to college from being suspended for my poor grades, while I indeed had plans to do things differently, he did not fit into my initial blueprint.

Then one day, completely on a whim, Damien and I found ourselves alone in his dorm room, and Damien and I talked that entire night, right into the following morning. Suddenly, I didn't see him quite the same way.

Although that night had solidified us as friends, I

still didn't consider him as anything more than that; my physical eyes had not caught up to my emotions, and Alicia was still an obstacle in our path. I hadn't experienced real loyalty from too many of my female friends in the past, but I knew what it was like to have someone like the same person I did. So, as long as Alicia was pining away for him, I considered him to be off limits in a romantic sense.

But I did enjoy the time I spent with Damien, and soon I found myself calling his room to speak to him just as much, if not more, than Shane. Something about Damien was different from any man I had ever met. He was so nice. He was so focused. He was so talented. He was so considerate. He was so healthy. More than anything else, what really stood out was that he was the only guy I knew who really knew what he wanted out of life and lived like he had no time to waste. Perhaps that's why when I asked him for the billionth time why he didn't approach Alicia for a date, he responded with, "Because it's not Alicia I'm interested in."

When I say that I didn't have a clue concerning the object of his affection, I mean it.

"So, who are you interested in? What's her name?"

"Her name is Shellie."

Shellie? Shellie. Wait, Shellie? Wait a minute—that was me! I was flabbergasted. Damien liked me? The chance of that happening never crossed my mind. At this point, the major reason was that, based on the discussions he and I had about women, I never considered myself to be his type. When it came to physical stature, I figured Alicia would always be a man's choice over me. She had long, wavy hair, a glowing complexion, huge breasts, and straight A's. Hey, I'm not kidding. She had a stack of trophies and tiaras to prove it. Me on the other hand, I had … none of those things. Not a one.

Don't get me wrong. Damien was attractive—just not my kind of attractive—and at this point, I was so carnal minded that all I saw was his light skin, slightly shorter stature, and love for the studio rather than the basketball court. To me, these were liabilities rather than assets. That's what happens when you don't invest your time wisely into the things that really matter. I had already experienced the tall, dark, and athletic. All it got me was pregnant and devastated. It's sometimes hard to see when you're in the dark.

Alicia certainly was no help. As she saw us growing closer, soon rumors were soaring about how I had betrayed our friendship and took her man. Although most of the lessons discussed in this book will be concerning the things men have taught me, here is one lesson a woman taught me oh so well. No woman can take a man away from you, especially if he was never yours nor had the desire to be yours in the first place. It's a harsh reality, but one that will spare you a lot of whiplash from unnecessary neck rolling in the future if you take heed.

Still, for a moment, I battled with my friendship with Alicia versus my developing fondness for Damien. After he confirmed that he never had any intentions of being with her, I erased Alicia from the list of don'ts when it came to why I would not take my relationship with Damien further than friendship. He still had a ways to go, but he persevered and did what a man had not done for me ever. He pursued me.

I'd be lying if I said he didn't put up a good fight, and I'd be lying even more if I said that after a while, he was breaking down some of the walls that my experiences with David and Michael had built up.

Damien wore his feelings on his always-creased Polo sleeves; it was refreshing to know someone so sensitive, but I didn't know how to handle it. He'd often buy me roses, cook me breakfast, or ask me out on spontaneous dates. But what really hooked me line-and-sinker was that he was a man who saw beyond my Coke bottle figure to the inside of my very being—my childhood abuse, my past relationships, the loss of my two unborn children, my fear of being hurt again. In the past, all men wanted to do was unclothe me. Damien used his love to cover me up.

It was not long before I found myself falling in love with Damien for reasons I had never loved anyone before. It wasn't because of how he looked, but who he was—a good man ... not a perfect one, but a good one, and that was the best thing for me at that time. Our relationship had its flaws, as all relationships do, but without a doubt, up until that time and for many years that followed, he was the best relationship I ever had—not just with a man, but with a human being. Because I could count on one hand the times we actually slept together, premarital sex had not spoiled our communication (although there were challenges— fornication always brings challenges) and because he came from a healthy home, he introduced better ways of communicating—whether we agreed or disagreed with one another. Until him, I didn't know what it was like to have someone know everything about me and love me anyway. Sure, there were things that needed some very fine tuning, but Damien was not into changing me, just improving what was already there; that's what a love relationship is all about. Not only did he love me, Damien celebrated me. For the first time in my life, I saw the definition of I Corinthians 13 in living color.

But remember, I was still wounded. Sadly, often it is the victim who in turn victimizes others. These days, whenever people ask me to explain my relationship with Damien, I usually can sum it up in three words: Hosea and Gomer. Do you remember that story in the Bible? If not, check it out, but the gist of it is that Hosea was a man who was married to a whore who he had to buy back over and over again to prove his love to her, because she didn't have much for herself. Change the names to Shellie and Damien, and you have a modern-day tale, minus the marriage and streetwalking. See, it wasn't so much that I was a physical whore, but an emotional one. I did whatever it took to get affection and attention rather than money, and that sometimes meant at the expense and risk of other people's feelings, including Damien's.

He stuck by my side anyway, often telling me, "I see something you don't see. I see that you are beautiful." Sometimes he would say that while smiling, other times through teary eyes, but it was always with confidence. I never did grasp the full picture of what he saw in me then. I wish I had before I lost him.

November 3, 1995, just one semester before he was to graduate from college and one month (to the day) after his twenty-first birthday, Damien died in a car accident that still leaves me baffled. He was at a gas station, and he left his car in neutral while paying the cashier. When he saw his car rolling into the street, he ran out to catch it and slipped on a water grid, and the car rolled on top of him, ultimately taking his life. That's strange enough in itself, but the story goes deeper than that. Much deeper.

Since our friendship began, Damien told me he believed he was going to die before he was thirty. That resolve always made me feel icky inside to say the least, but because I had yet to experience a death of someone who was young and close to me, I chalked it up to his own quirky paranoia and my own usual denial. The weird thing is that he never seemed scared about it, only resolved—so resolved that the summer before he lost his life, he dreamt about his impending death while interning in New York at Sony Records (he was studying recording industry management with the hopes of being a music producer).

"Baby, all I know is that it is going to be really quick," he would express to me sometimes over the phone in the wee hours of the night.

"Damien, I don't want to talk about that. You'll be fine. We have a lot of life ahead of us."

Looking back, I wonder if he was trying to prepare me, perhaps even more than he needed me to console him. Until I get to heaven, I'll never know, but that will be the first thing I ask him after the hugs and tears of our reunion, which will probably take a couple of eternities.

You would think, with how great our relationship had become, that I would have some really great story to share about the last moments we spent together. Well, actually, I do. A couple of days before he died, Damien asked me to marry him—but not in the traditional "on one knee with a ring" kind of way. It was better.

"Shellie, do you believe I'm your husband?"

"Why are you asking me that?"

"Because I need to know; I'll be graduating from college soon, and the only way I will stay in Nashville is if I know there will be something here for me other than work. That will make it worth it."

I told him that I loved him, and yes, I considered him to be the one with whom I would spend the rest of my life. We both knew we needed more time to begin our lives as singles before finishing them as a married couple, but that night was the moment we confirmed that someday we would be together as husband and wife. It had been a long struggle, but I had finally gotten to the point where I believed I was deserving of such a king as Damien. I started acting like the queen I was destined to become, and it was manifesting in a myriad of ways.

Just one example was the fact that it had been many months since we had been sexually intimate. If we were going to do this, we both agreed that we needed to do it right. I am so grateful that was not something he and God had to discuss in the last few moments of his life. Guilt only makes the grieving process worse.

Now that I think about it, in those last several months, we barely touched at all, and yet I felt so much closer to him. Finally, I was experiencing real intimacy, and I was being touched where it counted—the depths of my soul.

My newly discovered royalty was starting to change my whole approach to life, to me. At Damien's persuasion, I exchanged chemically straightened locks for my God-given birthright—a short, natural fro. At Damien's suggestion, I exchanged some of the clothes that showed my body for the ones that revealed my beauty. At Damien's request, I consciously worked on bettering my relationship with my family and my grades. Ironically, I had gotten so used to his directives that on that early Friday morning in November, at Damien's instruction, I listened to the last few words he would speak to me as we listened to Mariah Carey and Boys II Men's "One Sweet Day."

"I hate that song," I said while looking up at the stars.

"Why is that?" he asked.

"It's too morbid."

"Why? 'Cause it's talking about death? Shellie, if there's one thing you really have a hard time dealing with, it's reality. If you would learn to accept reality for what it is, things would be much easier for you in life, and death is a part of reality."

At the time, I found his recitation morbid and unnecessary. Just several hours later, I discovered it was amazingly prophetic. After getting out of his car and exchanging the routine "I love yous," I walked away from the man I would never see alive again. Just a month before, Damien went home to Chicago for the first fall break our school had ever had, claiming he needed to see his family—just because. The day he died, he spent the majority of it calling friends, both locally and abroad, claiming he was checking in—just because. At that time, my mother was working on a project in South Africa, but had called me early that morning wondering if anything had happened on our side of the world that would explain the sick feeling in the pit of her stomach—just because. That night, after Damien didn't call at 10 p.m. as he promised he would, I figured he got caught up with one of his friends—just because.

I will never forget the phone call that would later send me into a relapse of monstrous proportion. It was a homecoming weekend at another school, and I was at my house hanging out with some friends, when I returned home to dozens of voicemail messages. No one said what they were calling for, just that they needed me to speak with them as soon as possible. I called the person I spoke to the least first.

"Shellie, how are you doing?"

"I'm fine. What's up?"

"So, you're okay?" the guy on the other line asked, puzzled.

"Yes," I said, trying to rush the conversation. "Why wouldn't I be?"

"My God," he said after a long pause. "You don't know, do you?"

"Know what?" I asked, still oblivious to the sadness in his voice.

He paused. "Damien passed last night."

I promise you I didn't think I heard him right. I repeated what he said in my mind at least one hundred times in those next few seconds. Did he say that Damien passed? As in died? He couldn't have. I just saw him. Then I thought about the fact that he always kept his word, yet I never heard from him the night before. Then I thought about the fact that the only voice that was not on my voicemail was his. Then I thought about the last conversation we had and the ones that had preceded it concerning what he believed was his fate. Oh my God! Damien died!

My house was packed with loud conversation and laughter at the time, and after I processed what was said, I found myself laughing as well. I don't know why exactly. However, soon the obscure laughter changed into screaming and crying louder than I was even used to hearing myself. "Damien's dead? What? Damien's dead?" I said that over and over and over again, alarming everyone, including me. My boyfriend, my best friend, the man I said I would marry just a few days before, was gone. This was one blow I didn't know if I was going to be able to bounce back from. Years later, in some ways, I am still healing from the shock and sadness. To me, he had been the one.

I remember the time Damien and I met again—this time, not in his car or dorm room, but at a funeral home. I'm glad we were able to have some moments alone. Some of his friends had rented a bus to take to Chicago, but my mother wanted me to fly instead. She loved both me and Damien, and she didn't want me to endure any more stress than what was necessary. I was grateful for her discernment. I needed time alone to say my good-byes.

I stood there, looking at his face for what seemed like hours. I wanted to be angry with him—what were you thinking, chasing down a car, Damien?—but his face looked so peaceful. Although I knew I would never again hear his voice in my lifetime, in his death, he still had a way of comforting me as he did in our life together.

Although he never shared with this family the premonitions concerning his premature death, I later found more confirmations that he had felt that way for quite some time. He had also told his roommate Shane, and when his mother shared with me some of his memoirs from high school, I realized that while he said he would attend college, work for Sony Records, and meet Quincy Jones face to face (all of which he did accomplish), he never said he would graduate, get married, or conceive a son who would mirror his light skin or slightly shorter stature, to which I had finally grown accustomed.

When Damien had returned to school his senior year, he was more attractive than I had ever seen him. He had been working out and had exchanged his glasses for contacts. He had some of the most beautiful eyes I had ever seen. Actually, I think they had always been there, but it had taken me this long to actually see them. I would've given anything to see them again.

why not the prostitute?

Proverbs 4:2 states, "Above all else guard your affections. For they influence everything else in your life. Spurn the careless kiss of a prostitute. Stay far from her. Look straight ahead; don't even turn your head to look. Watch your step. Stick to your path and be safe. Don't sidetrack; pull back your feet from danger. For the lips of a prostitute are as sweet as honey and smooth flattery is her stock in trade. But afterwards only a bitter conscience is left to you, sharp as a double-edged sword. She leads you down to death and hell."

No one respects the prostitute
No one accepts the prostitute
But why not
Why not the prostitute?
At least she values her body enough
to receive some form of compensation
Why not the prostitute?
In the heat of July,
we're all walking around half-naked, and in midwinter
we're wearing even less
Our desire to be seen
overshadows common sense
For even a prostitute wears a coat
while waiting outside for her customers
Yet we refuse to wear one while standing in line at a club
Why not the prostitute?
At least if she gets a bad weave,
she is not trying to pass it off as her own hair
If she's wearing something that is too tight
or too small, it's so ridiculous
that you know it was not an oversight
If she's a size 16 and squeezing into a size 6,
it's simply because she
feels like it, and not because she's in denial
of her God-given physique
Why not the prostitute?
Because of her "For Rent" billboard on the outside,

as opposed to our "For Lease" sign on the inside
Because her soliciting is not as subtle as ours
Because someone commits to us
for three months rather than five minutes
Because her mouth says she's wanting
while our eyes say we're needy
Why not the prostitute?
Because she's in some cheap hotel
The back of a car
Behind a building
The client and her customer
in those same hotels and behind the same buildings can hear
many of us in the heat of the moment
Often leaving them behind moments after we got there
Why not the prostitute?
Because she is not worried about
whether he has a girlfriend, fiancé or wife
Because she walks with him proudly
as opposed to our ducking and dodging
Because she, unlike us, does not have the decency
to inquire of his
marital status before engaging
in a relationship with him
Why not the prostitute?
Because she's big on conversation
Because she's not always interested
in telling men what they went to hear
Because her time is not free, it must be earned
Because she can get the same man
with secondhand shoes, that we can with
Stiletto pumps
Because she can at least get him
to be honest with her about his intentions
Because she uses sex to get dollar bills,
rather than dinner and a movie
Because she does not mistake physical gratification
with emotional intimacy
Because he physically leaves her afterwards
instead of mentally leaving us during
No one respects the prostitute
No one accepts the prostitute

But why not?
Why not the prostitute?
Perhaps some of us are no more than the prostitute
Perhaps some of us are in denial
of the similarities between the two
Perhaps the only line of distinction
between the two is the name
For Proverbs 31:10 states, "A capable, intelligent woman—who
can find her? She is far more precious than jewels and her value
is far above rubies or pearls."
Why not the prostitute?
Do you realize your worth?
Why not the prostitute?
You can't be bought, you must be earned
Why not the prostitute?
You're exceptional by far
Why not the prostitute?
Do you know how valuable you are?
Why not the prostitute?
'Cause there's similarities in the two
Why not the prostitute?
We often share their point of view
Why not the prostitute?
Because we criticize our own infirmities
Why not the prostitute?
Because there's some of her in me
Because there's some of her in you

© Shellie R. Warren, 1998

chapter six
inside my brokenness

Numb. That's the only word I could use to really describe how I felt after losing Damien. Despite the strong face I had put on in front of our family and friends, soon it was becoming too much to bear. When Damien held my hand, I felt safe, and when he held me in his arms, I felt protected. Come to think of it, I never really thanked him for either one. He who had once been a huge presence in my life and a reason to reconsider living a life of sexual suicide had now become a distant memory. I tried using those recollections to carry me through, but it just wasn't the same. And it never would be again. Who was going to love me now, and if the answer was no one, where was I going to a least get a hit of love every now and then to make me feel that life was worth living at least one more day?

There's a real danger in not directing your questions specifically to the source of all the answers. If you don't ask God, you will either outsource yourself, or worse yet, anyone who can provide you with the quickest response. There's a warning in the New Testament of the Bible concerning what happens when you drive one demon out of your life. If you're not careful, several more will come and leave you more devastated than you had been with the one (Matthew 12:43-45). For me, these demonic holds came in the form of several men—none of them mine, but all of them willing to be with me for at least a few hours at a time for a few months or so. One was an athlete, one a senior in high school, one a senior in college, one a Muslim, and one a preacher's kid.

This period of my life was probably the most degrading. I once remembered hearing a friend of mine's grandmother say, "Women are sitting on a million dollars and giving it away for a Happy Meal." Shoot, I wasn't even getting that much for my time and attention, although in almost every way, I found myself to be the one spending a fortune.

As I look back on these five men, there were certain things they all had in common. They were all attractive and ambitious with good educations and great conversation. The icing on the cake was that they had cars, a little spending money, and no kids (at least that I knew of), which made them the cream of the crop wherever they went. Word to the wise: When you are in your early twenties, you tend to not look for much more than that, because you don't know you're supposed to; sadly, you think your age makes you too grown up to listen to the older women who try to tell you the average should not be considered exceptional.

Everything is progressive—even sin—so Faking It 101 prepared me for Mad Drama 101. I know this for a fact because it was during this time of promiscuity that I should have seriously considered taking up acting. I was acting like I was happy, acting like I was in control, acting like I enjoyed being sexually intimate (actually, "involved" may be a more appropriate word), and acting like I didn't mind being the other—and at times, the other other—woman. Without noticing it, I had invested so much of who I was—or at least who I wanted to be someday—into Damien, that when he died, in many ways, I died right along with him. This reality ended up haunting me and those around me for quite some time.

Damien was the only person who made me feel like I had more to offer than my figure. As a matter of fact, most times, he was perfectly content with holding my hand as we watched a movie in his room or hugging me while we watched planes take off at the airport. He listened to what I had to say, no matter how deep the secret, and he constantly reassured me that my past did not dictate my future. He wouldn't let it. I missed that. I missed him. I had gotten so used to his voice guiding me, and the silence of death was so blaring, that I searched for someone, anyone—even if it was five men who belonged to someone else—to say something, anything, to distract me from the pain of the loss I was experiencing. Even if it was only for a moment. Even if it was just background noise.

During this time of grieving, I had become an expert when it came to lying to myself, so I developed a real knack for telling lies to others. For starters, I would consciously gravitate toward men who were in relationships with other women, while telling them I preferred it that way. The major reason I did this was because I was still suppressing some serious low self-esteem issues from childhood that resulted from things said to me and about me. As a young adult, I still believed I was the "big lipped, buck-toothed, ugly girl with nappy hair and bowed legs" who would never get a date, let alone a man of her very own. Sure, Damien's presence in my life was beginning to change all of that, but it was years before I saw his death as anything other than another man leaving me for something else. For me, the grave was just a technicality.

So, I made it my goal in life to go after what people

said I would never have—even if, and especially when, it belonged to someone else. I mean, if I could take someone from someone else, I must be more desirable and not as ugly as people once said I was, right? Maybe not on the outside.

Although the fine guys appeared to always be taken, I merely saw that as a speed bump on lust's highway, and nothing—especially one of their girlfriends—was going to slow me down. My chance at true love had passed. It was now full-speed ahead, even if I was moving faster than I was prepared or created to handle … even if it meant I would crash and damage my self-worth severely in the upcoming several months.

Now sit tight. This is where things get interesting, and if you listen carefully, you just might learn something that will keep you from having my testimony. The first valuable lesson I learned from being involved with people already in relationships was this: Cheating is always dishonest; therefore you cannot trust a man who will cheat on you with his girlfriend. In return, they cannot fully trust you either. I don't care how much time you spend together, how great they say the sex may be, how many of their secrets they tell you, or how long the affair lasts. A part of them—and you—will always question their integrity because of their willingness to put their relationship, their character, and these days, their life, in jeopardy just for some sex (actually, the more appropriate phrase may be "for some more sex," because most guys are usually still sleeping with their girlfriends while they're sleeping with you).

The second thing I learned is that these kinds of men rarely care about the satisfaction of the other woman on any level. Even the things they do to you are usually for them, whether for their ego, their reputation, or their own distorted need for reassurance because of what someone told them they were or weren't in their own childhood.

As a direct result of my involvement with the Muslim, the athlete, the high school senior, and the preacher's kid, and the lack of involvement with God or myself (I was mad at both of us at the time), I told one of the biggest lies to some of them that I ever told in my life. I told them I was pregnant. That's right. During this time, by the grace of God, I was never impregnated, but I told them I was anyway. The weird thing is, I had gotten somewhat used to being pregnant in the real world, and I had also grown so accustomed to pretending these guys were my real boyfriends, that after telling that lie, I believed it as much—if not more—than they did. The various stresses from my lifestyle often caused my periods to become irregular, and because I was unsafe more than I was safe when it came to using protection, whenever my period didn't come when I thought it should, I would immediately assume I was pregnant and then begin reliving the moments when I actually had been pregnant. I didn't want to go through it alone, so when I felt really used, really scared, or really alone, I would draft some of them to experience those feelings with me.

This actually wasn't logical, it was sick, but I wasn't aware of how sick I was at the time. A pregnancy was the most dramatic thing I could come up with, and so I told the lie more than once—never making any apologies for it. The way I saw it, they never noticed or perhaps cared that I was faking orgasms, so I casually (if you can call it that) placed pregnancy (with plans of getting an abortion) on the list of the other lies I was telling. And why not? On our late night fast food runs, they never offered to pick up the tab, but oftentimes expected me to; after a few months, that could really add up. I mean, my friend's grandmother said I was worth more than a burger and fries, right? I figured this way I would get my money back, or at least half of it ($200). They didn't care about being honest or faithful to themselves or their girlfriends, so why should I be concerned with telling them the truth? They didn't care about me, so why should I care about them or how those lies may have possibly affected their psyche even to this day? I figured that to leave me broken and alone was just as horrible as leaving them with the impression that I had once been the mother of their child, even when I never had been.

Time, healing, and forgiveness—of others and myself—has caused me to really research the root cause of my made-up pregnancies, and this is what I came up with. Looking back on my first real pregnancy, there was barely enough time to emotionally heal from its termination before I found myself repeating the cycle all over again with the second one. Although I never saw or felt physical evidence of my unborn children, I knew they had been there, inside of me. At times, those thoughts were emotionally killing me to the point that I no longer felt good about anything. Not one single thing. The father of my firstborn was now fathering his own daughter, and the potential father of my second had been more concerned with keeping me a secret than coming to the aid of my maternal wounds. Several months later, it appeared that they were moving on and didn't care about what I was going through. But I was going through excruciating emotional pain, even if I didn't know how to show it in a way that would be beneficial to me in the long run at the time ... even if it meant making matters worse by bringing more people into the equation unjustly.

My distorted revenge—in the form of false pregnancies—was really my unhealthy way of dealing with what I had never really dealt with before—my loss. The two fathers of my two unborn children had never been there with or for me on any level (emotionally, physically, or financially) during my abortions, so I used some of my current lovers as stand-ins. They were going to do what the real fathers couldn't or wouldn't do, even if they had no other choice. The reality is, many of us manipulate those in our lives (although perhaps not as extreme) to mask or medicate our own pain, although we may not be ready to acknowledge or admit it. We make them pay for things for which they should never be held responsible because we are too scared, too jaded, or too unhealthy to confront the individuals involved. But just because a lot of us do it, it doesn't make it any better. Regardless of what those men did to me, or what I allowed them to do to me—they shouldn't have been held responsible for the make-believe pregnancies I conjured up in my mind while we were playing house late at night. So, I am taking this time to apologize. Do you remember me saying that victims often victimize? The way to stop that cycle is to heal the victim inside, not create other victims on the outside. It took years for me to come to that conclusion, but I have finally arrived.

Anyway, back to the other lessons learned. During this time of licentious living, the saying, "You teach people how to treat you," also started making sense (well, at least more sense than it had before. Remember, there are still several more chapters to read following this one). I always resented these guys for treating me like a doormat, but it never stopped me from lying down for them. This brought the term "call girl" to a whole new level, because whenever they called, I would come running, and after they got their fill, I was left emptier than before they called. In a letter to one of these guys (which I will share with you later) I wrote, "Sex is designed to bond you to another regardless of the circumstances." Some of these guys lasted only one night, while others lasted for months and years to come. The bigger they were in my mind, the harder my heart felt when the rendezvous finally came to an end. I thought I could handle it, but when it comes to being with people who don't belong to you (which is anyone other than the mate God gives you), you never can, because you were never created to.

This is where the senior in college comes in. During this time, he was a giant in my mind, so you already know I was in for a real heartbreak. We'll call him Jerry. I'm sure it won't be a shocker to you when I say that Jerry was six-foot, three-inches and chocolate, with pearly whites and great conversation to match. I once read somewhere that your first sexual partner usually sets the tone for all the rest. Although most of the guys were physically similar in one way or another, David and Jerry had some similarities that should have been my first clue to run faster than Forrest Gump ever did. I met Jerry one Martin Luther King Jr. Day at an event for which we were both volunteers. Actually, he got my attention at another function four months before, and although we caught eyes a couple of times, I didn't seem to leave much of an impression on him at the time. I guess our second chance meeting was the charm … or rather, the curse.

All day, Jerry and I found ourselves flirting with one another. After some light chitchat, I discovered he was attending a school that was about forty-five minutes away from my house (at this time, I was living at home again). We exchanged phone numbers and spoke that night. And the night after that. And the night after that. That following weekend, he and his roommate came down, and we all went to the movies. I was the one who paid for our tickets. I guess that should have served as my second warning, huh?

No matter. He made up for it by holding my hand throughout the entire movie. I couldn't remember the last time I went on a date with someone I actually liked, liked me back, and claimed me in public all at the same time. I was so grateful to him that several hours later, I slept with him. Actually, I wish someone could find another catch phrase for those kinds of experiences, because in most cases, sleeping—and especially sleeping over for the entire night—never takes place.

I always remember the first time with every guy I have been with distinctly, and Jerry was no different. Let me put it to you this way. Up until him, I always saw who was about to enter my body and spirit at the time they were doing so. In Jerry's case, I didn't—I couldn't, because he had kinkier ideas up his sleeve from the very beginning. Looking back, our sex life often set the tone for the rest of our relationship. There were so many things he did that I never saw coming. Of all the things I've been through, whenever I speak publicly on sex and relationships, I often say it was Jerry who provided me with much of the material I have to talk about. I don't have much to thank him for, but I will thank him for that. His craziness may make me a very rich woman someday.

Anyway, in the weeks to follow, Jerry and I spoke every day, and I would see him virtually every weekend. However, we rarely went out beyond that first date. The rest of our time together usually consisted of him wanting us to imitate acts he saw on late-night cable, and me mistaking it for the romance shown on daytime television. During this time, I was actually on the pill (most of the time anyway), although I was seeing the doctor more than I ever had. If it wasn't bladder infections, it was yeast infections. Amazingly, I never received a report of an STD (that comes later down the pike). Although he considered our acts of passion to be lovemaking, at times before, after, and during, Jerry actually scared me.

He was a sex monster. The scarier thing was that soon I found myself becoming his alter ego. Although I wasn't always happy, I didn't want him to become bored, so I did all he requested—sometimes even before he could even get both of his feet in my door. I won't lie, there were indeed moments when my flesh felt fully satisfied (isn't that what temptation is all about?), but those moments were becoming fewer and farther between (that's what the consequences are all about). I didn't care though ... well, not that much. He had taken me to places on a more consistent basis than any other man had before, so if I had to sit through five excruciating experiences to get just one of those peaks of pleasure, I was willing to do so—both in and out of the bedroom. And that's just what I did.

Now remember, when it came to one's dating status, I always found myself in similar circumstances, so in addition to Jerry being physically my type, he was also relationally my type—he had a girlfriend. I'm not sure when he ever spent time with her, because between his classes, his job, the frat he was pledging, talking to me throughout the week, and seeing me on the weekends, you would think the only time he had left he would use to sleep. But after months of X-rated sex, and my credit rate dropping due to my making his bills a

priority over mine ("Shellie, can I borrow $100? My
car just got towed." "Shellie, can I have $50? I need to
buy an extra book." "Shellie, I need $200. Don't ask
me why."), I came to discover that he was juggling
more than two women—more like six or seven. And as
disgusting as that may sound, I do have some insight
into why.

One night Jerry and I were talking on the phone,
and he shared something with me that I will never
forget. He told me the story of how he lost his
virginity. He said that he remembered his older brother
locking him up in a room with a strange girl and not
letting him out until he had sex with her. He was very
young at the time. That took me back to the "first time
theory" concerning sex that I had read and mentioned
earlier. If Jerry's first experience was basically a rape,
no wonder he was so rough when it came to sex, and
no wonder he was so hard on himself and me when
things did not meet his expectations. There was no love
in his first experience, so why would he give or expect
it now?

It takes a mature person to think through that
process. I was still very immature at the time. Almost
one year into the relationship, I found myself farther
from God and in deeper debt—in every way—than I
had ever been. If someone would've asked me why I
was with him, I wouldn't have been able to come up
with one good reason. But if I told someone the *E!
True Hollywood Story* of our relationship, I'm willing to
bet they would be able to provide me with a mile-long
list of why we needed to be apart. I'm sure God sent
me three billion warning flags during that time, but I
will share with you the third and final one that I can
remember.

If there was anything positive that was happening in

my life during this time, it was that I was developing
my writing skills. Aside from sex, writing was the only
escape I had from the constant pressures in my life.
Lord knows I had enough content at this point, and
soon rants and raves turned into poetry and prose.
At first I was only reciting these things to myself, but
soon I was provided with an outlet—a local joint in
Nashville where soon I became a house poet.

The very first piece I had ever written ("I'm Single
and That's Alright With Me") received a standing
ovation, and soon I was known as the relationship
writer. Most of my pieces were about self-esteem and
self-worth, and I must admit, the words were beautiful,
although I did not believe them yet. But we'll get to
that in another chapter.

Anyway, one night I sat down at a table next to a
sistah. She was cute and pleasant enough, but initially
I didn't pay her too much attention—that is, until she
asked me a very simple question that suddenly made
my life even more complicated.

"Excuse me. Where did you get that key chain?"

At first, I wasn't even sure which one she was
referring to. I was collecting them at the time.

"That one. The one of the man's face."

She was referring to the black wooden key chain
of a man's profile that I had bought while visiting my
mother in South Africa. I had given an identical one to
Jerry because I thought it looked so much like him.

"I know a guy at school with one just like it," she said
in a matter of fact tone.

"Really?" I was curious to see where this was going.
"What school do you attend?"

When she told me, I shared with her just how small
the world seemed to be, because that was where my
boyfriend went.

"Jerry? Your boyfriend is Jerry? That's my boyfriend."

Okay, I know what you're thinking. Technically, Jerry was never really my boyfriend, and you're right. But up until now, the only people in his world who I had seen or spoken with were his male friends, so to me, in our world, a woman other than myself did not exist. Until now.

This sistah of mine went on to share that she had been with Jerry for six months, but was on the verge of breaking up with him because she caught him cheating with not one, not two, but four other women. That was some shocking news in itself, but what really stood out to me at the time was the fact that Jerry and I had been together almost a year at that point, and he said he had been with his girlfriend since he was a freshman. That meant that the girl sitting in front of me was no more his girlfriend than I was, and suddenly I was no longer the "other woman," but the sixth person in the long line of many.

When I confronted Jerry with the information the girl had shared with me—how she found out he had borrowed some money to pay for an abortion with one gal, how he had gotten in trouble on campus for hitting another woman who was confronting him with rumors of at least two other women he was sleeping with besides herself—the first thing Jerry did was pit the blame on the two of us, claiming we were two immature girls who were trying to ruin his life as well as his rep.

If there was ever a time I felt totally and utterly played, it was now. Don't get me wrong, any time you sign up to play the role of second best, you are always played, but with the other guys, I knew what I was getting into—and had a good idea of what they were

getting into as well. To say this wasn't the case with
Jerry is putting it mildly. I'm sure you want to hear me
say that I immediately kicked him to the curb, and I
did … for a few months anyway.

In the eleven months I was committed to Jerry while
he was committed to everyone else, I learned several
lessons about hurting men who use sex as an outlet,
but the main thing is: Every man needs a good male
father figure in his life. If that figure isn't there, there's
an outstanding chance he will look to things like his
peers and the media to define his manhood. Most of
Jerry's friends came from broken homes—just like
him—drank alcohol, smoked weed, and sold a little
on the side on a regular basis—just like him—saw
nothing wrong with recreating porno flicks with their
significant other—just like him—found it cool to
have several women on the side—just like him—and
believed it was everyone else's responsibility to make
them feel better about the hand they were dealt in life
when it was not all they expected—just like him.

I've heard many people say it takes twenty-one
days to break a habit. Even though Jerry and I had
ended our "non-relationship relationship," perhaps
that's why it was a good solid year before I got Jerry
completely—well mostly—out of my system. Although
we didn't see each other all that much after breaking
up (or rather, breaking it off), I didn't live through
one full month without hearing the deep, smooth voice
that made me all warm inside, even if I was finding the
memories of our relationship leaving me ice cold more
and more.

A wise man once said, "When you realize that you
are getting less out of something than you are giving,
you will leave it alone." When it came to positive
things—things that made me a better person—my

relationship with Jerry left me as much in the negative as my bank account. That's not to say he didn't give me a lot of things. He gave me humiliation in front of his friends, who knew I was just one in the pack as he introduced me as "his girl" for my benefit and their entertainment. He gave me stress as I tried to figure out how to pay for gas and purchase groceries after donating money to whatever his emergency of the week would be. He gave me several contusions — internally as well as externally — after sharing moments of what I mistakenly confused as intimacy just because he called it making love. Let me take this moment to say that even if you have been in a consensual sexual relationship with someone, you always have the right to say "no," and if you find yourself with someone who mistakes force for foreplay and your screams for cries of pleasure, it's rape. Don't let him tell you otherwise.

It took a while, but I finally got to where I didn't allow his smooth voice and syrupy lies in the form of seductions to touch any part of me, physically or otherwise. I was strong enough to leave him alone, but too weak to be by myself. Soon, someone else would come along to fill the void. I was certain of this fact, because at this point, I had become an expert on timing. Bad timing.

revelation

You walk in, he grins—
Mesmerized, captivated, motivated,
determined to win your attention, so...
You just know how this will go
See, you're a queen, a woman,
the mother of children, visions, dreams
And since you've caught his attention,
he must have seen these things Sure, you're fine from head-to-toe
Hair laid, dressed to a tee, he'd have to be blind,
deaf and dumb if he could not see
But you're hoping that he won't just be
another causality in the war of fleeting passion and lust
See, you've learned, been burned,
earned the right to request, expect, demand

More than a "Hey Baby" or pat on the behind
Childish antics such as these are not worth his energy,
your time
Why?
'Cause Sistah Girl, you're fly,
and knowing that takes you high above
Shallow compliments, quotes from songs,
plagiarized poetry, tired pick-up lines
Lies, lying, being laid
Been there, done that, and memories now quickly fade,
and you can tell
'Cause you've changed,
exchanged visual stimulation with verbal proclamations
Knowing that your mind is a terrible thing to waste, and this fact
You don't debate or second-guess
by undermining your inner beauty
With half a dress, low-cut shirts, mini, non-existent skirts
You don't have to flirt like the rest
Showing your breasts, instead of your intellect
See, you've passed the "Cheap Sexuality" class,
and this is just a test
So ...
You walk in, he grins—
Mesmerized, captivated, motivated,
determined to win your attention

As well he should
But he'd better think about his game,
what he says, how he says it
His motive and meaning behind it
'Cause your standards go far beyond his number and a drink
Brotha, don't even talk unless you think, ponder,
re-evaluate the situation
'Cause whatever you do could make or break your ego
Don't you know you can only take her where she chooses to go?
So ... take your time, make up your mind,
see to it that you're just as fine—mentally—
and please go forth with creative determination
'Cause Brotha, whatever you say will be just another
confirmation to this revelation
And then you won't have to hear her say ...
I'm sorry were you speaking to me
"Hey Baby" is not my name
What gave you the impression
You could approach me in a way so lame?

So what am I doing tonight
The answer sure ain't you
I'm not interested in a quickie of any form
Whether it's conversation or the "one night stand" norm
You're inquiring why I'm so mean
I'm just ignoring your petty play
Mean is not what I'd call it
I simply have nothing meaningful to say
Why?
'Cause I don't know you
And to be honest I'm not impressed
I can tell by the way you stepped to me
That you'll holla at anything in a dress
So now I have a chip on my shoulder
Well as if your opinion matters
Just because you find me attractive
Does not automatically make me flattered
But don't think I'm discrediting your efforts
Or pointing you toward the door
I'm sure if you keep at it
Someone will give you what you're searching for

'Cause if there's anything I've learned
Is that men will use what's worked before
It's a shame that women answer to "Baby"
That they don't know they deserve much more
The respect must be demanded
And jerks will push as far as you will go
Men will learn how to approach a lady
If we would not settle to go with the flow
So now you say "Excuse me"
And your tail's between your legs
You say you've got too much pride
And that you are too proud to beg
I say pride is what we have in common
That's why I don't stand for any mess
If you want the joy of my company
You'll have to give much more than less
So good luck "Mr. 'Hey Baby'"
You'll get out what you put in
What you came with was a bunch of nothing
Persevere and try again
You want to know my problem
My solution would help you more
Next time you approach a lady
Learn her name not after but before

© Shellie R. Warren, 1998/2000

chapter seven
inside my third pregnancy

As had been the case with so many others, Reggie was very attractive. He brought a whole new meaning to tall, dark, and handsome—my favorite combination. He was at least six-foot, six-inches, his skin was a smooth, deep chocolate, and he had wavy, ebony-colored hair. He was beautiful.

Of course, because I still hadn't seen the ridiculous pattern I was making for myself, I came to know him the same way I had gotten involved with every other guy I'd been interested in—different location, different time, but the same results. This time, I was at a frat party with some friends, and one of my girlfriends spotted him in a crowd.

"Girl, he's fine," she said in her deep New Orleans accent.

He was fine, but after looking him over, I decided to place him on my "way out of my league" list and responded to her declaration in a way that would make her think I didn't care about him and make me think that was the truth.

"He's alright. He ain't all that."

She rolled her eyes and quickly proceeded to the dance floor to do some further investigating. As I had so many times before, I remained on the sidelines and watched her play the field. A couple of hours later, she came out sore-faced and empty handed.

"He blew me off. He said something about having to hang with his frat brothers tonight, but that it was really nice to meet me. Can you believe that?"

To be honest, I could. No offense to my friend, because she was c-u-t-e in her own "short-n-sassy" kind of way, but he was way beyond such a simplified four-letter word. He was Godiva chocolate at its best—a fine and rare delight—and it would take more than a "what are you doing tonight?" to capture or keep his attention. And although that fact was obvious, I still didn't like the look of defeat on my friend's face as she walked away. Her facial expressions reminded me of how I had felt internally so many times after wanting something I too couldn't have. I wasn't bold enough to approach Reggie for myself, but I was certainly audacious enough to serve as her unsolicited spokesperson. How dare he ignore the mediocre just because he was magnificent. How dare he.

"Hey, I didn't appreciate you blowin' off my friend in there," I said as he was leaving the venue.

My accusation alarmed him at first. "What are you talking about? What friend?"

"The short girl in there was trying to talk to you. Couldn't you tell she was interested?" Sure, my hand was on my hip and I was talking up a good game, but inside, my heart was racing. For one, he was towering way over me, and for two, he really was a sight to behold; the fact that he would take the conversation even this far was making me like him even more.

He smiled. "I didn't blow her off. I simply told her I had to go, and I do have to go—I'm hanging out with my frat brothers tonight. Who are you anyway?"

Ah, so an interest was piquing in him as well. Sure, he may not have been looking down with the same physical admiration with which I was looking up, but something was making him stay in my presence just a little longer—even if it was nothing more than curiosity. Reggie and I stood there talking for what seemed like eternity, but in reality, it was probably no more than five to seven minutes. The conversation ended with me getting his phone number, and this should have been my first sign that I was on the wrong side of love's tracks—again.

For the next several weeks, Reggie and I conversed over the phone. At first it was an exchange of courtesies … you know, "Where are you from?" "What are you studying?" but soon things got deeper. Looking back, if there's one thing I can give Reggie credit for, it was that he was very open and honest about his priorities: his family, his schoolwork, his frat, his basketball team, and his girlfriend—not necessarily in that order, although in time I came to see that his girlfriend continuously remained on the bottom of the pile.

I was finding myself to be more and more intrigued by him with every conversation—and we soon began having more and more of them on a regular basis. But because I was always starving for attention from guys I liked, any crumb he could give (a return call, a compliment, even a request for my advice) held me over until the next time I would hear his voice. Soon the phone calls were not enough. Discussing the intimate details of his life caused our casual relationship to become deeper as well, although it seems we were swimming in two totally different emotional pools. He was finding me to be a confidant, while I was considering him a potential future boyfriend. Soon, the fact that he had a girlfriend never even crossed my mind—even though he continued to talk about her, and I continued to listen.

One night we were engaged in what had become somewhat routine conversations, and the topic we had strategically avoided—for whatever reason—came up: sex. To be honest, I can't really recall who brought it up, but I'm pretty sure it was me. I had always prided myself in having no skeletons and being an "open book" when it came to the intimate details of my life, but regardless, the end of the conversation immediately resulted in me gassing up my car and taking a two-hour drive to his school.

Funny how that trend began. Once again, I was the one making most of the long-distance phone calls, and once again, I was doing most of the work when it came to the relationship. I believe things were odd for both of us when our eyes met again for the first time. No longer were we just two people at a party, but for better or for worse, we had become friends. For better or for worse, we had become intimate. For better or for worse, I was in his dorm room and would be spending the night.

I tried to act at least moderately naïve, like I didn't know what a college-aged athlete had on his mind at midnight. I mean, I might have been his friend and all, but we could have stayed friends over the phone. I knew it; he knew it. And soon, we did it. Of course, I had gotten so used to faking pleasure with many of my previous partners that I had fooled even myself into believing I enjoyed the experience as much as he seemed to. For a few weeks, we tried to act like it was working, "it" being the fact that we were friends, he had a girlfriend, and we were having sex. And because we had come to know each other pretty well on a mental and physical level, I once again confused that with real intimacy and told myself and him that using a condom wasn't necessary. Because I wasn't his girlfriend and he didn't feel the need to lie to me about the dirt he was doing, I believed him when he said he could count the times he had ever had sex without one, and because he was an athlete, I knew he had been tested for STDs, and a baby was the last thing on his mind. Sure, the fact that he was having sex with me meant there was a pretty good chance I was not the only one with whom he was cheating, but because we had shared so much, and because I knew so many of his secrets, I felt I could trust him. If he said I was the only one with whom he was having unprotected sex, surely he was telling the truth ... never mind the fact that he said he loved his girlfriend, and yet he was lying to her about sleeping with me. Never mind the fact that not once did he proclaim any feelings he had for me. I still believed—or rather wanted to believe— that there were no lies between us.

I mean, there was the lie I told him every time we were together, and I would act as if I was having as much fun as he seemed to be having. Sure, there was the lie I told when I said to him repeatedly that I could handle being his sex toy and not his intimate partner. Sure, there was the lie I told myself when I said that having him touch me even just for a few minutes would fill all of the empty spaces in my heart. But those were necessary evils—ends that would justify the means— and because once again, there were no immediate physical consequences to our reckless rendezvous, I chalked them all up to little white lies—the ones that couldn't really hurt—and I ignored the huge warning signs that were flashing before me.

WARNING: You have been here before.

WARNING: Aren't you sick of being in relationships where you have to do all of the work?

WARNING: It will only be a matter of time before

you end up heartbroken, pregnant, or both.

It was only a few months before I crashed. Once again, I was holding a pregnancy test with a positive result on it. My third pregnancy. For a few moments, I even wondered if I had gotten pregnant on purpose. I don't mean that I told Reggie I was on the pill when I wasn't, or that I consciously made sure we had sex while I was ovulating (although in hindsight, it's obvious I did), but I do wonder if a part of me had gotten so attached to Reggie that I didn't want to risk losing him, at least a piece of him in some way. But most of all, I had already aborted two other children — maybe this was my subconscious way of finding out if I could still conceive.

Ironically, unlike my first pregnancy with my "first-love thug," and my second, which was a toss-up between my first love and my first lust, I didn't have the same level of fear as I had before when I received the news. For one, I was older, so the opinions I once feared didn't scare me as much. Secondly, I had lost so much (my innocence, my first love, my other children, Damien, me) that I took the consequences — loss — a little more seriously at this point. But more than anything, although I wasn't in love with Reggie, I was almost obsessed with the possibility of having him, a man just like him, or a piece of him in some way. Even now, when I look back on all my past involvements, Reggie is someone for whom I will always have an affinity. He was intelligent, attractive, funny, and sweet. He treated his family with the utmost love and respect, got along well with others, was active in his church, and cared about people's feelings, including my own.

I didn't want to hurt him. Perhaps that's why I waited until after his finals his senior year before even telling him I was pregnant. In the meantime, I told a girlfriend of mine who begged me to go to full term.

"Shellie, I believe you are carrying a son and that you should name him Jeremiah," she said. "Remember, before the womb, we are called and chosen, and there is a plan and purpose for your baby's life."

For about two weeks, whenever I would see or talk to her, she would greet me and the life growing within me. "Hey Jeremiah, I can't wait to see you."

She also pleaded with me to write Reggie a letter telling him I was pregnant and not to speak with him directly until I was into my second term, hoping that by then, I would be more attached to the pregnancy. "Don't let him talk you out of it, Shellie. It's not his decision or yours. It's God's."

I didn't listen. The week of Reggie's graduation, I broke the news that broke his heart—or at least his ego. Amazingly, the tables turned, and he was calling me every day, several times a day ... begging me to terminate.

"Shellie, you're not ready for a child. I'm not ready for child. I would say the same thing to my girlfriend, but you and I are not even in a relationship. Please don't have this baby."

I didn't know if I wasn't ready. For the first time, I actually thought, *Is it really my call on whether or not I am ready to be a mother?* After all, at this time, I was in my mid-twenties, I was clear on who the father was and liked him, and a part of me was ecstatic that God had not taken away my ability to get pregnant. However, one thing that had not changed was the fact that I didn't consult God on what He wanted me to do. Deep down I think it was because I knew what He wanted me to do—suck it up and deal with the fact that my disobedience and carelessness got me into this predicament, and now I needed to lean on Him to carry me through. Before being Shellie and Reggie's baby, my child was His, and so He should be allowed to have the final word on the outcome.

But Reggie kept pleading, I kept listening, and one Memorial Day weekend, I returned for my third termination. I didn't recall seeing so many people from so many different walks of life before. It was midday on a Friday, and there were women in business suits wearing wedding bands, a pre-teen crying on who I assumed was her mother's shoulder, and even a couple of faces I recognized on campus. To this day, I have kept a pact with one of the girls I knew pretty well at school, vowing to never reveal her secret.

Personally, very few things made this experience different, except for the fact that for the first time, the father of my child accompanied me to its funeral and paid for the procedure (actually, one of his college friends who was currently playing in the NBA did). Other than that, everything else about the abortion was a blur.

In times past, the medication usually left me pretty out of it, but this time, my adrenaline was higher than ever. Reggie helped me into his car, and on the ride home, he asked me if there was anything I needed. I told him I wanted to stop by the mall to buy my brother his birthday present.

"Shellie, the nurse said you are to take it easy for the next few days," he said, startled.

"I'm fine."

"I really think I should take you home."

"I don't know if she's ever been through this, but you definitely haven't. I know what I'm doing. I want to go to the mall."

For the next few hours, I went from store to store

searching for a gift, all the while taking glances at Reggie and noticing the puzzled look on his face. After leaving the mall, at my request, he took me to my brother's father's house, and I handed Jonathan my present. "Jonathan, this is my friend, Reggie. Reggie, this is my brother." They exchanged courtesies, and I handed Jonathan my gift. To this day, I can't tell you what it was. I told him I loved him, wished him "happy birthday," and was finally off to the place I had been scared to go—my house, the place I had been inside just hours before while my baby was inside of me.

Reggie dropped me off at my house. I could tell by his nervous pacing that our time together was coming to an end. "I have to get on the road. I'm going to my parents' house for the weekend. Call me if you need anything. May 22."

May 22. The day my third child was placed to rest and the first time that Reggie was able to express any kind of emotion directly toward me. Later, he told me that it was his way of saying that he loved me and that he would never forget that day. I'm not sure if what he was feeling was love, gratitude, or relief, but whatever the sentiment, lying in bed, looking up at the ceiling, I thought, *What a high price to pay to have him feel something for me.*

It was then that I could feel the anesthesia setting in. I couldn't feel a thing.

letter to an ex-boyfriend

"Though the companion of your choice was in all other respects worthy, yet he has not accepted the truth for this time, he is an unbeliever and you are forbidden of heaven to unite yourself with him.

"To connect with an unbeliever is to place yourself on Satan's ground. You grieve the Spirit of God and forfeit His protection."

There's not much to say after that, is there? For months now I've been grieving the loss of you and begging and pleading with God to give me you. One day God led me to a passage out of a book entitled, Testimonies on Sexual Behavior, Adultery and Divorce. How can you start off on the wrong foot and not expect to be on a crooked path's journey? You can't, not without God's help, and I obviously was not inquiring of Him as of what to do. If I had, I wouldn't have experienced as much pain as I did.

I really loved you.

Despite the other women, the lies, the selfishness, the moodiness, the broken promises ... I still loved you.
When God finally revealed to me what love truly was about, I became confused. You mean love's not supposed to hurt, I'm not designed to feel lack in a relationship, and love is actually a healthy thing?

But I loved you, and it felt anything but good. And if I'm really honest with myself, the only time I felt loved, wanted, desired, appreciated, was when you were in my bed. I thought we were making love, but what we were making was a mess. We used the illusion of sex to avoid pain. The pain of the disappointment from life's experiences, the pain from the abandonment of those closest to us, and the pain of the uncertainty of our future. For the brief moments of pleasure in a sexual relationship, we could escape reality.

What we did not realize in the law of nature, is that sex is designed to bond you to another, regardless of the circumstances. The more we hurt, the more sex we would have,

and the bigger mess of our lives we would make. Now I was
bonded to something God never gave me,
I simply took.
A year later I still get the shakes as if I'm a junkie getting off of
coke. I know it's no good for me, know it will ultimately kill me,
and yet sometimes I feel like I will do anything and risk anything
for that one last hit.

"God, I know he doesn't love me as I deserve. I know he has
other women. I know he's not faithful to You, so how could I
expect him to be faithful to me? I know all of this, God, but
please influence him—no, make him love me."

God would remain silent, and the eerie void was suffocating, so
while an alcoholic runs to the bottle, I would run back to you.
Just one last conversation, one last kiss, one last night in your
arms, and everything would be all right.

But it never was, and it never could be, because I was asking
God for love and you're not it. God promised to give me the
desires of my heart, not the aid to my addiction. I was so fixated
on you, I had forgotten what I asked God for way before there
was a you.

Way back when my parents divorced, when I was introduced to
Barbie and Ken dolls. Way back when a guy I had a crush on for
six years told me that I was ugly.

Way back then, I asked God for love, and He has shaken
heaven, earth, my heart, and this relationship to deliver just
that ...

True love, and this ain't it.

© Shellie R. Warren, 1998

chapter eight
inside of the cycle

At the time, nothing seemed as hard as getting over my third pregnancy. I know this, because the days that followed were some of the lowest in my entire life. As a matter of fact, the only death that came even close to hurting as much was the loss of Damien—and even he was a matter of the heart, not my bloodline.

I found myself continuously calling Reggie to see if he was going to keep his vow to always be there for me—that our relationship did not end once I got off of the surgical table and his genes got out of my DNA. He always answered, he always listened, but I slowly found myself resenting him for not listening right, not talking right, not doing right. This was all wrong. The more he comforted me, the more I wanted our baby back, and the more I got up to change my pads due to the residual blood from the abortion, the more I realized I could never go back. I'd never know if our baby had my eyes or his nose. If it was a he, would he love to write like his mother? If it was a she, would she love playing ball like her dad?

These were questions I had never asked myself with my other two children, and more and more, I could see that it was because I was no longer the same person. Abortion was no longer a solution to a problem, but a symptom of a disease that was killing me, as well as my kids. And I wanted to die. I mean, what kind of woman

deserved to live if she would kill her own? At this
point, I was too emotionally tired and spiritually devoid
to wait on an answer from Reggie, myself, or God.

Especially God. Oh, my God. I didn't even want to
know what He thought of me. How could a Father
love someone who would kill His own children—even
if the murderer was one of His own as well? It was all
too much for me to take ... so I decided not to take it
anymore. One night, I found myself returning home
with a pack of sleeping pills. Suddenly, breathing was
more than I wanted to endure. Sure, I knew suicide
was wrong, but God didn't see one sin as worse than
any other right? Abortion, suicide—it was all death to
me and to Him at this point. Shoot, I figured the only
reason why He hadn't killed me Himself was because
He was keeping me around a little while longer to
suffer. And who could blame Him?

It was getting dark, and I turned on the television.
Then I turned it off. I got in the bed. And then I got
out. I was restless and exhausted all at the same time.
Was it selfish to kill myself right in my own mother's
home? Who would find me? My mother was out of
the country, so how long would it take before my
stench would take over the house? More questions
without answers, and they were only making matters
worse. The only place I found to be even remotely
comfortable was the corner of the bedroom, and there
I sat and cried and screamed, only to cry some more. I
wanted my baby back, and there was nothing I could
do—except join it in death.

I opened the pack of pills and held them in my moist,
sweat-stained hands while wiping my tear-stained face.
I was really going to do it. I had contemplated it so
many times before (even before the sex and abortions),
but this time I was consumed with the thought. Who

knew what consequences were waiting for me on the other end, but just to have a couple of moments where I didn't have to hear my own conscience, to me, was well worth it. At the very least, I was sure Reggie would be grateful, because it would mean he would get a much needed and well-deserved break from my phone calls.

Just then, I heard a laugh. I smiled, thinking, *Wow, I can still do that?* But as I listened harder, I realized it wasn't coming from me. It was too low, too obnoxious, too wicked to be coming from me. I looked up, and straight in front of me was an out of focus silhouette crouching before me, laughing. The scariest part was that I wasn't scared. Actually I thought, *Perhaps I won't have to do this myself. Someone else can get the heat for ending my life.*

I tried to see just who was finding my pain to be so hilarious, but his features never did become clear, although his laughter was getting louder and louder inside of my head. Just when I thought he was going to reach out and touch me, my phone rang, and he vanished.

Who would be calling me now? I thought. *Should I answer it?* Tired of being powerless in any of my decisions, I picked up on the fourth ring. I don't know if I said "hello" or not.

"What are you doing?" a sultry voice said on the other end. It was my girlfriend Stacey—one of the last people I would have ever expected. Sure, we spoke from time to time, but I couldn't remember the last time. All I knew was that we hadn't had a conversation since before I was pregnant. Regret filled my lungs again, and I was finding it hard to breathe.

"Nothing."

"Nothing?" she repeated. "You're never doing

nothing. What's going on?"

"Nothing," I heard myself saying a second time. "I'm just really tired. I've gotta go."

"Listen, we haven't spoken in a long time, and you know it's not me to just call for no reason. The least you can do is humor me and hold a conversation." That was Stacey. Very self-consumed. But this time it was to my benefit.

"I'm just going through a lot right now, Stacey. I'm not much company." Out of nowhere, more tears started to fall. I didn't know where they were all coming from. I couldn't remember the last time I had something to eat or drink. You would think I'd be severely dehydrated by now.

"Shellie, what is going on?" Stacey asked, this time more alarmed.

"I'm just so tired. I … I don't … I'm just so tired."

"You just don't what?" she repeated.

"I don't think I want to live anymore," I said, barely above a whisper.

I've heard many people say that at moments like these, you are not really wanting to take your own life, you are simply crying out for help, but I promise you that in those brief moments, I honestly believed Stacey would be the last one to hear my voice.

"I'm on my way. Don't do anything until I get there, you hear me?"

I heard her, but I wasn't listening, and I definitely wasn't making any promises.

She was telepathic, I guess. "Do you have someone you can speak with until I get there?"

I had been depressed before, but up until now, no one knew about my termination, and I didn't want anyone to know.

"Shellie … do you hear me? Who can you call to stay

on the phone with you?" There was urgency in her
tone of voice.

"Reggie."

"Call him. Now."

I don't think I've ever told Stacey this before, but
back then, she had a way of intimidating me. I did
what she said, and Reggie picked up on the first ring.

"Reggie, I don't want to live anymore. I killed our
baby," I said through my snot, snorts, and tears. By
now he was used to it—the actions, not the words.

"Shellie, don't talk like that."

"I hate myself. I want our baby back."

What can you say after someone makes a statement
like that?

"May 22, Shellie. I said we would get through this
together, and we will."

I hung up the phone. I didn't want to get through
this. I wanted my baby back. Why was I taking this
so hard? The first time I had an abortion, I returned
to work the following day. The second time, I
went out clubbing with my friends that very night.
Looking back, those were probably also cries for
help too, because each time, I remember the doctor's
recommendation of staying off of your feet for the
first couple of days to lower the risk of a potential
hemorrhage while recovering from the procedure.

But I had never been at the point where I couldn't
get out of the bed, or where I didn't see life after
my babies' deaths. I picked up the phone on what I
thought was the first ring, but Reggie confirmed it was
more like the tenth.

"Shellie, you nearly scared me half to death. I was
about to call 9-1-1."

I just sat there completely silent. "Shellie. Shellie.
You there?" There was fear in his voice. I was there,

just barely, but by then there was a knock on my door. I was going to see another day. I never again saw that dark figure who was laughing at me as I contemplated my fate. I hope he gets around to reading this book someday. The joke's on him.

I was on the slow road to recovery in those months that followed. My outlooks on sex, death, abortion, and relationships were changing drastically—although I did have a few relapses (of the sex) from time to time. On some days, the necessary steps needed for a full and permanent transformation—talking to God, reading the Word, restructuring my social circles, forgiving myself, releasing the past and my old habits—were more than my mind or body was willing or wanting to take. Yet slowly but surely, I was finding something other than sex to serve as my rehabilitation.

Without a doubt, I know God gave me a gift when it comes to writing. I say this because over the course of my life, there have been so many times when after writing a piece and reviewing it, I would be amazed—almost as if I was reading someone else's words. How could such a wounded and broken spirit create such poetic words of reconciliation, forgiveness, and self-love? I definitely didn't feel that way, and yet, somewhere within, my spirit was making a comeback over my flesh. God used words to create the earth. He was using words as well to recreate me. At the time, I was doing a lot of writing and reading, but very little listening and doing. When you want a life-changing experience in your life, you have to fully follow through.

It did wonders for my self-confidence to receive positive feedback from my peers at the poetry joint I was regularly attending at this point, but it also did my heart good to hear other people recite their creations as well. Finally, I was fitting in, I mean really fitting in, and I couldn't remember the last time that had happened to me. For a few hours every Sunday evening, I was in the presence of people who were just like me—different. Some had long locks; others had huge fros. Some wrote about social and political consciousness; others conveyed words of wisdom, love, or peace with themselves and others. There were even those whose appearance and recitations were sexually aggressive and borderline offensive, but they received applause just the same. In that dark room dimly lit with candles and incense, it wasn't about getting everyone to like you for how you looked or what you did; it was about gaining everyone's respect simply for being.

In no time, a family of poets had developed. There was Stacey—the sultry, five-sentence statement reciter; Kay—the sexy and in some ways downright crass crooner; Mya—the tortured soul who very finely walked the line between religion and abuse; James— the young man who used the stage to hurl insults at women in every which direction to mask the pain of being used by them; Keith—the daring, in-yo'-face performer who was all man in a skirt; Donna—the quiet wallflower who left you in shock and at times disgust as she shared her detailed memoirs; and Ramone—to this day, one of the most talented writers I have ever seen step up to the mic.

I had never understood groupies until I met Ramone. I mean, how do you fall for someone you barely know, other than their fifteen minutes of fame while performing onstage? Ramone was cute in his own kind of way. He had a beautiful cinnamon complexion and great muscle tone, with a bald head and a designer name urban kind of style. He was far from ugly, but nothing to write home about. Besides, by now you should know what I went for, and he certainly didn't fit the bill. Ramone was five-foot, ten-inches on a good day, and I never saw him throw any kind of ball, whether it was on or off the court. He never went to college, let alone finished, and the closest he came to Christianity was his upbringing; he was a practicing Muslim. He was so not my type, and I found comfort in this in a way. Other than Anthony and Austin, I didn't really have any platonic male friends, and I thought it would be nice to have one who shared my interests.

But something looked different about Ramone when he took the stage. Suddenly, the short, bald guy without the formal education seemed larger than life. I'd never seen or heard anyone quite as convincing as him, no matter what the topic. No wonder he left women—including myself—mesmerized as he recited his poetic ode to the ladies at request from time to time. However, by this time, I was getting a little more hip to the game. He was good, and I made sure to give him a standing ovation with the rest of the crowd, along with a "good going" at the end of the show, but that was about it. Besides, from the look of things, he didn't need any more female accolades. It was not rare that after a performance, Ramone would leave with a pocketful of numbers and a different girl on his side as he walked to his car.

"You are such I pimp," I would tease, halfway serious.

"Why would you say that?" he would often respond. "I love women, but I don't abuse them in any way."

"You play them," I would retort.

"I am honest with them upfront, and I don't do anything they don't want me to do," he would reply. "Besides, why do you care? It's not like we're in a relationship or like you want to be. I'm short, bald, and not dark enough, remember? Chill."

It was these kinds of verbal matches that slowly but surely began to intrigue me. For everything I said, he had a counterattack, and when it came to the battle of the intellectuals, I had not encountered a worthy opponent in quite some time. He stimulated my mind in a way none of the others had. Sure, they had college educations, but he had real wisdom—the kind that came from living life outside of the classroom. Still, I thought he was a womanizer to the tenth power, so I kept my distance romantically while drawing closer to him emotionally. Soon, we found ourselves talking on the phone at least two or three times a week. I think we both found it a relief to have someone of the opposite sex to talk to without it being "pillow talk." He would ask my advice on his latest flavor of the month, and he would consult me on how to avoid being a notch on the belt for someone else. Ramone made me laugh, and more importantly, he made me think. Perhaps if we had left it there, he wouldn't have made me cry several times over.

I recall once taking a series of intimacy courses along with some other Christian singles. The married people who were teaching the course recommended that we split off into same-sex partners as we went through the class. The reason they discouraged couples of the opposite sex joining up was because they said too much sharing could encourage false intimacy. This meant that because you were sharing personal details of your life, you may have the tendency to think the developing bond was eros (passion) rather than agape (friendship). This is good advice. When it came to my relationship with Ramone, I should have applied it.

In no time, we went from random phone calls and

seeing one another on Sunday evenings to daily phone
calls and road trips (he lived about an hour away,
ironically in the same town as Jerry). Looking back,
even when I went to his home, we were rarely alone; it
wasn't that kind of party. I would usually go up there
for a cookout or house party that he was hosting, and
if he ever stayed at my house, it was with a couple of
friends after being too tired to take the drive back after
hanging out all night after the poetry reading.

We soon became what more people considered
to be brother-and-sister-like than boyfriend-and-
girlfriend-like. We both were know-it-alls, especially
when it came to religion, and to be honest, although
time and association were drawing me closer to him,
that closeness was what I considered to be our biggest
barrier. I had no desire to be in another pointless
relationship, and I remembered what the Word said
about being unequally yoked with non-believers. Here
was a man who shared my love for writing and the
arts. Here was a man from whom I learned as much as
I taught in conversation. Here was a man who ate the
way I did, didn't drink, and even observed the seventh-
day Sabbath. Here was a man with whom I never
argued and who never mistreated me or my body.
Here was a man who came from a good home (to this
day, his parents remain happily married). But when it
comes to having a successful relationship, 99 percent
of the truth just isn't enough. That was the first lesson
Ramone taught me. In our case, the 1 percent might
as well have been 100 percent. I was taught to believe
Jesus was my Savior, and Ramone didn't believe that,
and although I didn't know it at the time, later down
the road, I would severely need a savior in a very major
way.

I don't know if it was nostalgia or what the first

time Ramone and I discussed our developing feelings for one another. Although we discussed everything else, both of us had been internally debating the pros and cons of having a more-than-platonic relationship. We knew we loved each other in a very special and intimate way, but I wasn't interested in sharing him with other women, and he wasn't interested in giving them up. It didn't stop us from sharing our first kiss though. Although I remember my first sexual experience with every man I've been with, I don't remember my first kiss with most of them. But this one was special. It was soft, it was tender, it was gentle, it was between two genuine friends. And over time, it became toxic.

Next lesson, people. This is when I really learned that there is no real benefit to having a friend with benefits. If the two of you have decided to bring sex into the picture, you have crossed the friendship line, even before you do it, and there's no turning back afterward. A major difference between Ramone and my other escapades was that he told me he was in love with me. What made this worse than the guys who didn't was that he followed "I love you" with "and I don't want to be." I never really heard the second part; I was so starved for the "I love you" part. I hadn't heard that since the day Damien had died, and until then, I didn't know just how much I had missed it. You think there's nothing worse than not having anyone to love you? Trust me, there is.

Ramone and I didn't know how to handle our newly discussed feelings, but believe me when I tell you the route we chose was all wrong. We wanted to find a way to keep things as they were before we shared those three little words that can do so much, but the damage had already been done. One illustration of how sick it was, was in the fact that for months (way before our secret confessions), he had told me about this girl who was stationed overseas for whom he had major feelings. They both discussed that they could and would see other people while they were apart, but when it was all said and done, they planned on sharing eternity with one another. The friendship side of Ramone wanted me to meet her when she came into town to visit, and I did. The undefined part of Ramone dropped her off at one of her friend's houses that night and returned to me and my bed.

If you're healthy, that will make no sense to you, but if you have ever settled for less than what you deserve, I'm sure you will be able to somewhat understand the compromise. Ramone and I were trying to find ways to keep it all. Instead, we ended up losing everything. There's a saying that crazy people are those who do the same thing expecting a different result. Technically, my middle name is Renee, but at that time, it should have been "Ridiculous." Here I was, back in the bed of someone who did not belong to me, back to compromising my principles for pleasure, back to being the one who was doing more giving than receiving, and several months later … back to debating the fate of yet another child over the phone. That's right—baby number four.

Sure, I was scared. I mean, even I had to admit this was getting pretty ludicrous at this point. But this time, I thought things were going to be different. This time, I was older—too old to use my age as an excuse. This time, I was actually having sex with someone I loved and who loved me back. This time, my baby's family knew me, loved me, and encouraged the pregnancy to go full-term. This time I was with someone who adamantly opposed abortion—or at least that's what he claimed when he gave unsolicited advice to his male friends when one of their girls was in trouble. Oh, but so often the shoe hurts when it's actually on our own foot. This time, when it was a matter of his blood rather than his opinion, he was like all of the rest. He didn't want it.

For the most part, Ramone had been a stickler for birth control, and at the time I had gotten pregnant, condoms were sparse, and my need was for satisfaction was great. We had gotten away with going without them a couple of times, so I figured that as long as he pulled out, it wouldn't hurt. Besides, to me, condoms made me like all the other girls with whom he had been. Since he loved me, I wanted to be different, set apart. I was. I was the first girl he impregnated. It was my fourth time having to share the news.

"Shellie, I don't want to have this baby. It's just not something I can handle right now."

Ramone had recently lost his job, which caused him to be in a real financial bind. He was going through a crisis of conscience when it came to what he wanted to do with the rest of his life, and the last thing he considered was bringing on something new like a child. Aside from that, being "friends with benefits" had taken its toll, and we both resented each other for numerous reasons. For Ramone, more than anything, it was because he felt like I had trapped him.

"And don't blame me for your mistakes. It's not my fault that this is not your first abortion."

Wow. As the conversation went on, his anger mixed with his fear, and confusion caused him to sound like all the ones who had preceded him. Sure, he claimed to love me, but his definition must have come out of something other than the Bible. As I stated before, he didn't claim to be a Christian, so I guess that's par for the course. At this point, it wasn't about his moral views; it was about his personal comfort, and the thought of a baby—our baby—was not something he wanted to deal with. So, he found termination to be the best solution. I guess he assumed I wouldn't give him such a hard time about it. After all, at this point, I was a vet.

"You don't want to keep our baby?" I cried.

"No, I don't. I do love you, Shellie, but we can't raise a baby right now, and when it comes to you and me, I don't know if we ever will. We can't agree on much these days. How are we going to be able to agree on raising a child?"

I've liked someone and lost a baby. I've lusted someone and lost a baby. I've loved someone and lost a baby. Like I said, I was ridiculously insane, and if I ever have to go to court on such charges as pregnancy termination, that is what I will plea.

December 4, 1999, I was right back in the place where I said I never wanted to return ever again. This time, it was a different city. I know God had a plan for all of my children's lives, but I think there was something extraordinarily special about this one, because this time, there were many obstacles in the way. When we arrived at the clinic, lots of protestors were outside the front doors.

"Ramone, that's a sign. We're not supposed to do this."

When we got out of the car, someone tried to assault me, and Ramone had to defend my right to walk through those clinic doors.

Again I said, "Ramone, that's a sign. We're not supposed to do this."

For hours we sat in the lobby looking at one another. My mind was racing. Suppose this child was to heal the wounds from my past? Suppose this child would rebuild the bridge between me and my mother? Suppose this child would give me reason to see my biological father on a more consistent basis? Suppose this child would be the avenue to helping me find my purpose in life? But more than anything else, suppose this child was created in sin so that it could lead his or her father to Christ? What was I doing? What was I doing, again?

By this time, my mother had remarried and moved to South Africa, but I remember her telling me something I will never forget, as I lay in the bed of recovery from what I hoped and prayed would be my last pregnancy and termination. I was through with saying what I wouldn't do. I was seeing more and more that I needed God's help to overcome my addictions—and yes, even abortion can become an addiction.

"Shell, these boys will always be able to have children. They don't deserve any part of your body, especially your uterus. You so want them to love you, but I want you to love yourself. Today is not the day you need to be preached to. You know right from wrong. God loves you, Shell. Take a bubble bath. Get your toes done. Do something to take care of you. Not one more man needs to be the reason why you are lying in the bed hurt and crying—before or after a pregnancy."

We still had a ways to go, but it was at that time that my mother and I started the healing process. For the first time in a really long time, she was there to soothe my wounds, and it did more for me than you could ever imagine. It wasn't about what I did; it was about who I was—her daughter and God's child. I didn't see it yet, but they saw something better for me—a man who really loved me. A purpose in all of my pain. A time when all of this nonsense would make sense. It hadn't happened yet, but rest assured, it was going to happen.

Ramone had a child by another woman a little over a year following our experience. As Sally said in the '80s hit, *When Harry Met Sally*, after finding out her ex-boyfriend of several years met and married another woman just several months later, it hurt to know that it wasn't that Ramone didn't want to be a father. He just didn't want me to be his child's mother. The cut from that reality has only recently healed.

Later, Ramone shared with me that while he tries not to live in a world of regret, he does reflect on that decision from time to time, wondering what would or could have been. Ironically, he's not alone. All four fathers have told me they have grieved that loss in some form or fashion over the course of time, assuring me that the solution was not as cut and dried as they initially thought when I shared the news with them.

One father said, "For months I sat in church and looked at a little girl who looked liked what I envisioned our daughter to be. She had a dark complexion and curly hair, just like me, and was loud with bowed legs, just like you."

Another said, "I didn't really take the time to think about the fact that was me inside of you, but a part of me died right along with it."

I don't know why, but God saw fit to let me live even amid the precious lives I had taken. I decided to take some time off and heed my mother's counsel and God's Word. You can't love your brother until you know how to love yourself. I was determined to find out what that really meant, alone. The memory of my past children and the lives of my future ones deserved at least that much.

i'm single and that's all right with me

I'm single and that's all right with me
Tell me, why is that a contradiction to you?
What makes you think that just because I'm an attractive
woman of intelligence, and over the legal drinking age, that I'm
incomplete without a mate?

What makes you think that just because my conversations
quench the thirst of many parched from the ignorance of dull
chit-chat and just because when you talk I can respond on
whatever the topic, whatever the level, whenever the time,
that I've obtained my knowledge simply for your entertainment
purposes only? No, I'm single and that's all right with me

What makes you think that my present status is not a God-given
right, a woman's choice and a healthy decision?

Who told you that without a man, something's missing from my
life, and if so, what would that be?

Love?

I love myself, and more importantly,
I love the Lord
He told me when I delight in Him,
He will give me the desires of my heart

Security
I have everything I need according to His riches in glory

Intimacy
Now, how's a man gonna get to know me
when he doesn't even know himself

See, my Father told me that I am above a ruby's worth,
and a gem does not seek, it is sought, so why would I sell myself
out?

No, I'm single and that's all right with me

See, it's not that I oppose relationships,
it's that I detest codependency

Girl, as a woman I know it's not my role to chase after any boy
who professes to be a man

Esther 2:14 states that I am to wait on my king,
and when he's delighted in me, he will call me by my name

My Mama didn't name me Needy or Desperate
I am to be cherished, relished, valued, honored
It's not my job to convince him or convict him of that
My mate will already know it and consistently show it
He'll know that making love to me requires caressing my mind
before fondling my body

And he'll stay on his knees daily, not just to adore me, but to
praise the Lord for the virtuous woman he's found
So when you see me by myself, I'm not alone, I just know what I
have coming to me

I'm single and that's all right with me

© Shellie R. Warren, 1997

chapter nine
inside the end of the cycle

The devil never takes vacations. I can't tell you how many times I've heard someone say that, but it wasn't until my experience with yet another tall, rich, caramel-colored grad student by the name of Chris that I saw just how close to home that statement could really get.

My previous relationship had taken such a toll on my body, my mind, and my spirit, that for the first time since losing—well, giving—my virginity, I consciously got off the sexually active relationship cycle and pursued the single life. That meant no dating, no late night phone calls, no kissing, no petting, and more importantly, no recycling or searching for the next person with whom to do those things. The irony to all of this was that I was really happy being alone. I was really happy being with me.

During that time, I read books, went to the movies, and shopped at thrift stores. Now that I think about it, perhaps it was because I now had money, since I wasn't always spending it on someone else (hmm …). Anyway, I did what I wanted to do, when I wanted to do it, without worrying about what a man thought about it or how it would affect the relationship. And there was a real peace in that.

But more importantly, God and I began being intimate. I read devotionals on a daily basis and prayed more than once a day, which made me closer to Him and helped me become more sensitive about what I did, how I dressed, what I listened to, who I hung out with, and what He thought about all of that. In the past, I was so obsessed with what men thought about me that I never took the time to ask or care about what God thought, what He saw, or what He ultimately wanted for my life. Finally, I could hear God more clearly, and it was becoming evident in everything about me. People were taking notice … especially men.

However, even with all that had already happened to me, if there was one lesson I had not yet learned, it was relational discernment. While I was finally beginning to enjoy single living, deep down in the crevices of my heart, there was always a part of me that wanted to have someone to love. By this time, several of my friends were in serious relationships—if not married (or remarried)—so I'd be lying if I said I didn't dream of having a hand to hold in the mall or during a chick flick from time to time. I just knew that next time, I didn't want it unless the guy pursued me, romanced me, and then committed to me and me alone—a major feat when it came to me and my self-respect. Like I said, when it came to God, I was doing more listening, but I soon discovered that when it came to dealing with people of the male gender, I was still doing entirely too much talking.

I was several months into living in the luxurious lap of the single and satisfied when Chris came on the scene. At the invitation of a friend, I went to a spoken word joint, and there he was. He immediately caught my eye. He was one of the tallest men in the room, and as I have previously shared several times before, the tall, dark, and handsome are, without a doubt, extreme weaknesses for me.

For a while, he stayed in the back of the room and

watched all of the others on the open mic list recite their words of love, social consciousness, ignorance, and lust, but then he did something I wasn't quite prepared for visually or mentally—he recited an original piece as well. Wow, he was cute, *and* he was a writer. This was a combination I enjoyed. This was also the point at which I should have realized the devil himself had walked into the venue with the sole purpose of stealing the internal peace I had come to know and love. For clarity's sake, Chris wasn't the devil—bad timing, poor discernment, and not facing these things head-on are simply what the devil used as the foundation for what turned out to be a very unstable relationship.

At the end of the show, I went to the back to greet some of my friends who happened to be talking with Chris. My second warning flag should have been that these same people also knew Ramone. Birds of a feather flock together, right? No, this couldn't be good. I spoke to them anyway, and they introduced me to him. Chris continued to be what I wasn't expecting. He was more. He was better, and the real catcher was that he was totally unlike me. Chris was very soft-spoken, and when he talked to someone, he had a way of making them feel as if they were the only person in the room. Tall? Check. Handsome? Check. Poetic? Check. Polite? Check.

Still, he wasn't enough to get me to cheat myself out of the awesome relationship I was developing with me—yet. Besides, knowing my luck, he probably had a girlfriend or several "friends with benefits." Been there, done that, no thank you. As he began to speak to me, I decided to keep the conversation short, sweet, and to the point. Thirty minutes later, I left, but not without leaving him my email address at his request.

He was really something. No "What are you doing later tonight?" No "Can I get your number?" As a matter of fact, there was none of the undercover mack daddy garbage to which I had grown accustomed. All he wanted was my email address.

The next day I received an email from him as promised. And for several days, that was the only way we corresponded, although with each email, things became more and more personal. Salutations went from "Later," to "See ya," to those dang emoticons everyone uses to convey emotion over the Internet, and even those were transitional. At first he used smiley faces, but soon they became roses. As the women did in the '95 flick, *Waiting to Exhale*, I found myself taking a sigh of relief. Not long after that, he asked for and received my phone number.

After talking for hours every day, Chris and I finally agreed on a date, although looking back, I see that once again, it took very little effort on his part. We went to the twenty-fifth birthday party of one of my girlfriends, but first, he met me at a mall so I could buy her a present.

They say first impressions last the longest, but when it came to his appearance, I must say the second had the biggest effect on me. He was so handsome, with his turtleneck, leather jacket, and naturally curly hair, and he became even more appealing as he reached for my hand. We walked around the mall chatting about well, everything—too much for a first date. As I have previously stated several times, every relationship I have experienced has taught me at least one valuable lesson. What Chris taught me was that a woman should never tell a man what she wants in a relationship. She should shut up and let the man reveal who he really is, and then decide if that's something in which she wants to partake.

Hindsight can be a mutha. As we walked and talked about our past relationships and why they hadn't worked out, Chris asked me, "So, what are you looking for in a man?"

I don't know what excited me more—the fact the he asked, or the fact that he was awaiting my answer. Either way, it was something no man had ever asked me before, and I was more than eager to respond— even if I didn't realize that at the time. I told him I wanted someone who was attentive, intelligent, and spiritual. He immediately assured me that he was all of those things, and to this day, I am willing to vouch for the fact that he was all of these things ... to a certain extent. He was very attentive to his needs and how I could meet them. He was intelligent enough to manipulate me into thinking that everything that went wrong in our relationship was my fault, and that he didn't play any part in the drama. He was spiritual—so spiritual that I never saw him pray or go to church (only once with me in our almost one-year relationship), and I don't even recall seeing a Bible, although there was an E. Lynn Harris collection in his room ... but we'll get to all of that later.

There's nothing like talking and having someone listen to you—I mean, really listen to you. Chris did just that for me. I told him I loved pigs, and he showed up one time with a pink stuffed animal in his car. I told him I loved to eat fish, and he made some for me on several occasions. I told him I liked cuddling without it being an expectation of sex, and that he willingly offered. One of my fondest memories of Chris and me was when he took me and spun me around in a mall, persuading me to partake in an impromptu dance while listening to the overhead speakers. He was tenderly romantic, and I was getting very accustomed to this lifestyle.

Soon the emoticons on the computer changed from roses to lips, and the two-hour movie/mall dates became sleepovers. At first there was still no sex, but because we lived about an hour apart and he didn't want me on the road late at night, I would pack a bag and stay. It was becoming addictive to be in his presence, in his space, and I wanted more of it, of him. Soon our friendship became a relationship—a real one. According to me, he was my boyfriend. But get this: According to him, I was his girlfriend as well. It was a hot mutual love affair that soon sent a lot of people talking.

If you play with matches, sooner or later you will strike up the fire that will burn you. This fact included carnal passion. I don't know what made me think that I could continue to sleep in the bed with Chris and not sleep with him, but it was only several weeks after meeting him that this passion was ablaze. Looking back, I'm not sure if we were so much sexually compatible, or if it was just that I had gone without sex for so long that I thought doing it with him was the best thing on earth, but as with most people who fall off the sobriety wagon and back to their addiction of choice, I was getting run over several times a week—completely numb to the pain, completely engrossed in the pleasure. The cycle had returned in all its glory. And I was making no apologies for it—not even to me or to God.

It was weird. In many ways, my habits and I were the yin to Chris' yang. He was quiet. I was loud. He loved to cuddle. I loved to kiss. He was in grad school. I was a dropout. He was an aspiring writer. I was a professional one. He came from a two-parent home.

I came from a broken home. He and his mother were close. My mother and I were not. When I got angry, I would say why while yelling at the top of my lungs. When he got angry, he would mope around, pout, or sit in a dark room alone, not speaking for hours — most times with very little warning. He loved to decide what we ate, what we watched, and when we did these things, and because I was so used to being the doer in all of my other relationships, I loved letting him. Most of all, he was sensitive to his feelings, and so was I.

Soon Chris and I were finding less to talk about and more to argue about, which gave us more to make up about. It was not long before making up was all that we enjoyed about each other. Because sex had once again spoiled great communication, I found myself missing Ramone more and more. It's funny how the flaws of one person can make you forget the flaws of another. On one hand with Chris, he called when he said he would call and came when he said he would come. I never paid for dinner dates, and he always had thoughtful gifts for me at the right occasions. He openly claimed me as his woman, and he even took me home to meet his family. On the other hand, Ramone and I could talk about anything for hours, his moods were always consistent, and with all of the things I heard and knew about him — his selfishness, his arrogance, his inconsistently consistent resolve on religion, and his rendezvous with other women — there were certain things about him that I did not question, not once. I was finding myself missing that fact terribly.

I was still recovering from the battle wounds of my relationship with Ramone, so my interaction with Chris felt more like pulling the scab off of a newly covered wound than salve on a healed up scar. This

wasn't fair to either one of us. The more I saw Chris
for what he really was—a hurting and flawed human,
just like myself, the more I resented him for it, and
the more I missed Ramone. Soon, I found myself
accidentally calling my current boyfriend my ex-lover's
name, which in turn made both of us insecure. Chris
was wondering if I wanted to be with Ramone, and
based on Chris' cryptic moods swings, his secretive
phone calls, the way he responded when I told him he
looked just like his father, the nonchalant attitude he
had whenever we would discuss homosexuality, and—
to top it off—the rumors that were being planted in
my head about him and his past, I was wondering who
Chris wanted as well.

It wasn't long before we found ourselves not liking
each other very much, but the sex continued, even
despite all of my unanswered questions about his
sexuality. I mean, he couldn't be gay. He enjoyed
having sex with me, and deeper than that, I enjoyed
sex with him. I was no longer faking physical
satisfaction, just emotional contentment, so I was
willing to overlook the checks in my spirit as long as
my flesh was being satisfied. You would think I had
learned by now.

Then one day I received an unexpected phone
call: "Shellie, I'm glad you're in a relationship. I am
currently in a one myself, and I believe we are both
happy. That is not what this phone call is about. But,
given all that we have been through, I'm always going
to love you, and your safety will always be important to
me. There are rumors going around that Chris is gay.
You may want to ask him about it. Oh, and if he gets
you sick, I will kill him."

Ramone hung up. Despite the pleasure I was
experiencing with Chris, it was humiliating to have

my ex tell me that my current was a homosexual, so I pushed my libido aside in exchange for logic and confronted Chris with the information.

"I can't believe you asked me that," was his initial response. "You've slept with me, and excuse me, but you seem to enjoy it. How could I be gay?"

Keep in mind there was no "No. Who the heck told you that? Of course I'm not gay." No statements at all. Just questions. Not mine—his, and to be honest, I didn't know how to answer them. He was right. I did enjoy sex with him. And up until now, I had no idea that any man could pull of such a stunt—pleasing a man and a woman at the same time. What confused me even more was that some of the men who were the hetero in heterosexual never made me feel the way he did. Something wasn't quite right.

To this day, Chris has never confirmed to me that he was or is a practicing homosexual, but I will tell you what I do know about him. As of the last time that I spoke with him (about two years ago), Chris still had a horrible relationship with his father—a man who looks and, in many ways, acts just like him. Nothing he ever did was good enough for his dad, from school, to his choice career, to his appearance. Interestingly enough, he and his mother seemed to make a sport out of dogging his father out because neither of them received much affection from him. But more than anything, he never confirmed that he wasn't gay. Not once.

The scariest issue was that he and his roommate argued, gossiped, and made up more like lovers than friends. As a matter of fact, a couple of weeks after breaking up with Chris, another friend of mine—a delivered homosexual—asked me about my relationship while waiting in line at the post office. I'll never forget what he said about a man he met once.

"Shellie, I am so glad that you are done with him because … he was gay. Aside from his mannerisms, I can tell you the kind of men he went for. They are smaller than him, and so he can boss them around. They probably also have a girlfriend, but she is probably being used as a front girl, just like you. They …"

If you paid me a million dollars, I would not be able to tell you the rest of what he said, because his first four sentences were more than enough. Here a non-practicing gay was telling me that the man I chose to believe was straight—even amid some of the telltale signs—was gay as well. My God. I was not looking forward to being yet another statistic, but on top of everything else, I could now be one of those women who's had a down low brotha—you know, the men who sleep around with men but don't share that information with the women they are also sleeping with. It is because of these men that the toll of black women with HIV is on the rise.[1] A year ago, I was having the time of my life. Did my return to disobedience bring it all to an abrupt end? Was this the time I was destined to lose at the sex, life, and spirituality gamble?

I am blessed to say that as of now, by the grace of God, I am not HIV positive, but it hasn't been seven years since I've been intimate with Chris, either. Grace doesn't always cover up the consequences in life. But it was at this time that I saw, really saw, just how much the devil hated, I mean, really hated me.

Being abused as a child hadn't aborted my mission. A drug-dealing boyfriend hadn't aborted my mission. Promiscuity hadn't aborted my mission. The death of the man I thought I was going to marry hadn't aborted my mission. Even the abortion of my children

hadn't aborted my mission. So, as he so often does
with our vices of choice, the devil had to step it up a
couple more notches. He brought me a man packaged
in the wrapping of my choice—attractive, attentive,
intelligent, creative, single—and didn't show me
all there was to him until he was inside of me—
figuratively and literally.

And do you know what I did about it? I did what I
always did when the man in my life showed his true
colors—I tried to change him. I guess I had already
figured I was ahead of the game because this one had
actually been a formal boyfriend, so while we did break
up, I remained in contact with him—in all senses of the
word—about every two months for about six months.
That's right. Even with the warning signs (more like
sirens) going off, because I was so fearful of failing at
yet another relationship, I told myself there were still
some good things about him and us, and if he needed
love, acceptance, or sexual orientation therapy, I would
do my best to help him.

I know his friends were laughing behind my back,
because I was looking more and more like a joke to
myself. I had reached an all-time low with this physical
high. Not only was I having sex—again; not only was I
in a non-relationship relationship—again; not only was
I continuing to stay involved with someone for whom
I was losing more respect with every passing day—
again, but this time it was with a potential bisexual.
You'd be amazed where strongholds, codependency,
and the fear of being alone will take you. Nowhere and
fast.

So, what brought it all to a final end? One day I
went to see him, and he simply looked disgusting to
me. He was still tall, dark, and handsome, but there
was the residue of filth that was either all over him or

my eyes. To this day, I cannot tell you. I didn't know who or what he was, but what I found to be even more unsettling was that in knowing him, I didn't know who I was anymore, either. Our involvement with each other had become a constant game of "stick-n-gab," both physically and emotionally, and we were both wounded as a result.

But what really gave me the courage to walk out of his apartment without the courtesy of even a goodbye was remembering just where I had been before the night at that spoken word event, and so wanting to be there again.

1 Tamala Edwards, "Men Who Sleep With Men (AIDS Risk To African American Women)," *Essence*, October 2001, "Double Lives on the Down Low," *NY Times* magazine, August 3, 2003.

this doesn't belong to you

You say I seem cold and distant
Don't know what's wrong with me or what you should do
I say I'm fine and you should do nothing
I've come to realize that this doesn't belong to you

And what "this" am I speaking of?
I'll give you a list and you can just choose
My heart
My time
Most definitely my body
You haven't made a commitment
So this doesn't belong to you

My apologies for sending mixed signals
I've just realized my worth
My mind's been renewed
My vision's no longer distorted
My hearing's become more in tune

And what I've come to recognize
Is we share separate points of view
You think you are owed
I know you must earn
I was bought with a price
By God
Not by you
So this brings me to the conclusion
That this doesn't belong to you

For years you would denounce the "all of that" women
Saying they think they're better than you
Unaware of what I'm deserving
I would encourage your point of view

By giving you parts of me that are sacred
Belonging to one and never a few
I now see what those women were saying
They already knew that this doesn't belong to you

So now you wanna roll out the red carpet
And treat me like a woman of virtue
It's too late
You should have thought of that sooner
You took advantage of my ignorance
And yearning to be close to you

As a man you should have led me to this conclusion
But it's all right
I'm not gonna put this on you
You shouldn't be held accountable for what isn't yours
And I'm not
This doesn't belong to you

Believe me, this will help us in the long run
We're royalty and shouldn't act the way we do
A mere slave boy and peasant girl
Forgetting we're heirs to an abundance
In relationships and prosperity too

And since I'm a queen
I'm gonna start to flaunt it
Can't balance a crown on my head
And be on my back too
Personally, I find there to be no comparison
Sorry, but this doesn't belong to you

I hope you're not offended
But more than that
I hope you know what to do
Start with respecting your own body
Know there's a crown also waiting for you
That there's rarity in men who know they're deserving
Of a whole woman
Not just one part or two
Then maybe you'll start holding out and saying
"I'm sorry young lady, but this doesn't belong to you"

© Shellie R. Warren, 1998

chapter ten
inside of me

When my relationship with Chris came to a final
and complete end, I couldn't believe it. Once again I
had failed, and this time it seemed worse than all of the
other relationships combined. Sure, to the physical eye,
the consequences may not have appeared as severe, but
internally, I was a mess. The thought of ending up with
a potential homosexual never crossed my mind, and
even with all of the facts that had been laid out before
me, and even months after it ended, the thought was
still really hard to grasp. As scary as that possibility
may have seemed, what was really freaking me out was
that, for each time I allowed myself to fall for a guy,
the hole—the hole in my heart, the hole in my soul, the
hole in my body, the hole in my being—only seemed to
be getting deeper, which meant I was finding it harder
to get myself out on my own when the relationship
came to an end. Here's where the lessons about myself
come in, and I am pleased to say that here's where the
conclusion to my assorted tales begins. Better late than
never, right? Praise God for mercy.

First of all, let me get one thing straight. Although
most of what you've read has been, well, I guess
"heavy" would be the most appropriate word, my life
has not consisted only of the men I've liked, loved,
lusted, and lost. There have been some good times—
times when I have laughed out loud, times when I have

seen great movies, attended exciting concerts, and
visited fun places. As a matter of fact, I'd like to think
that my outgoing personality has given me a pretty
good sense of humor by default. Throughout all of my
pain, life has also given me some pretty good girlfriends
over the years who have stood by my side. They may
not have experienced as much as I have—or, they may
not be as willing to put it out there on paper—but they
have always supported and encouraged me along the
way, even when I didn't support and encourage myself.
As I have gotten older, while they have remained to be
physically beautiful, it is the inside that makes them
stunning. I've often heard that one is what they attract.
If that's the case, then I am eternally thankful.

Oh, and remember when I mentioned my two
friends, Austin and Anthony, from my freshman year
in college at the beginning of my book? To this day,
I am proud to say that they are still in my life, and
while they have always been in my heart, they have
never been anywhere else as it relates to my anatomy.
I know it has hurt them at times to witness all I have
been through, but they have been there, loving me,
nonetheless. When I lost my virginity, they were there
(not literally, of course, but emotionally). When I took
my first pregnancy test (that ended up being false—
and I should've heeded that warning, by the way),
they were there. When I lost Damien and all of my
children, they were there. And when I felt so low and
lonely that I tried to use one of them as a temporary
fix—he was there to refuse me because he saw beyond
that night into forever, and beyond my faults and into
my greater need. Thank you, Austin. It is because of
you and Anthony that I did not lose complete hope in
male relationships during those times. Ladies, strictly
platonic relationships can be real blessings, so listen

up: Don't try to make every good man your husband.
You may miss out on their real purpose in your life …
and really end up missing out.

Then there's my career — no, my destiny — and
while it may and does have times that are filled with
unpredictable ups and downs, I am doing pretty well,
even if I do say so myself. Without a degree or formal
training, I have met people I would have never thought
possible in a little bit of time, which has led me farther
down my life's road than I would have ever expected,
and at a much faster pace. Yes, in many ways, life has
been good to me, but that's not what this book is about
or the purpose for writing it.

The objective of this book is to share some of the
things that weren't so good, in hopes that in these
words, some would find a friend they could relate to;
others, a shoulder to cry on; and others, a voice in a
place within their wounded soul that they thought
had gone deaf or maybe even died. But more than
anything, it is for those who have yet to have someone
know them in the ways that I have shared with you
in these previous chapters. Hear me when I say that
whether it's Chapter 2 or Chapter 8, no one who's
not your spouse deserves to know you in the ways
I have shared, but hear this as well: I'm not saying
there is anything wrong with sex. I certainly don't
think that, but what I am taking this time to reiterate
is that marriage is the best environment for a sexual
relationship. There is supposed to be safety in sex,
not risks. It is to celebrate love, not challenge it. What
I have come to realize the hard way is that sex is an
awesome gift from God that is meant to be enjoyable,
but is also meant solely for married people, and with
good reason. As it states in Ephesians 5:22-31, women
are supposed to submit themselves to their husbands;

husbands are supposed to love their wives as Christ loved the Church (and gave His life for it), and in marriage, they are to become one flesh. Married couples deserve the satisfaction of sex because their commitment to one another and to God entitles them to it. The wife has made the eternal decision to submit to her husband, and the husband has done the same as it relates to his relationship with God. In marriage, submission to God does not stop; it changes. However, as a single person, anytime you decide to partake in pre-martial sex, you are putting that person and your relationship over God, which means you stop submitting to Him entirely; any time you do that, one way or another, things will go wrong, because you are placing your will for your life over His. Nothing good ever comes from that.

No, when I say that no one who's not your spouse deserves to know you in the way the men in my life have known me, I mean that no one deserves to be involved with you to a point that you would have to experience the things I have. Sure, the common denominator in all of these sick equations has been sex, but there are other variables as well: abuse, low self-esteem, loneliness, fear of abandonment, desperation, confusion, anger, bitterness, jealousy, resentment, lies, selfishness, manipulation, and the repetition of these things over and over again, because at the time, I didn't know I deserved better.

It took me a long time—too long if you ask me—to realize that the kind of love and intimacy God desires for my life will never breed such negativity, and that what I had been experiencing was not lovemaking at all, even if I thought I loved them at the time, even if a couple of them had said it back. Making love is not about what you can get, but what you can give. Sex without a commitment, no matter how many "I love yous" you say or hear, is really only about what you can get, because you are essentially saying, "I know this could hurt both of us, but my needs right now are more important than your potential pain." That's not love at all. It's unfair, unrealistic, and unsuccessful to expect anyone to take the place of God, but basically any time you break His laws for your personal satisfaction, you have set that person or relationship on a pedestal; you just made them a mini-god. Believe me when I say that when you try to make anything or anyone take the place of God in your life, you will be disappointed every time. Humans are not supernatural no matter how much they like or love you; that's God's job.

Just think about it. I have given you several scenarios that have all ended up with very similar unhappy endings: "Once upon a time, Shellie met a man" eventually ended with the closing chapter of, "And they lived unhappily resenting one another for many days, months, or years following the end of a relationship that should have never had a beginning in the first place." To be honest with you, I'm not really sure what the purpose of these men in my life was supposed to have originally been, but I know without a doubt that it was never so I could say, "I used to sleep with him," "I allowed myself to be used so I could feel loved," "I purposely hurt him because he hurt me," or "He used to be one of my babies' daddies." The Word says God desires to give us abundant life; this promise applies to the relationships we have with other people. Looking back, nothing but death and devastation came from doing things in my past relationships my own way instead of God's.

Trust me when I say that I did not share all that I

did just so you would know all of my business; no,
it was to prove that if you apply pre-marital sex to
any equation—casual sex, "friends with benefits,"
or dating (whether it's with or without intentions to
marry)—there will always be problems and many
times, very serious, life-changing, detrimental ones,
not because sex is bad; as a matter of fact, it's so great
and so powerful that you need God's blessing and a
marital covering to keep it from destroying you. God's
laws concerning sex and marriage are so you can be
protected in your pleasure. If God created it, don't you
think He would know how to use it better than any of
us?

I would know better than anyone that sex without
marriage is not meant to "hook you up," but hang you.
It has taken me longer than I would like to admit, but
I have come to see that God loves me so much that
He wants me to have the most pleasurable, the most
committed, the most intimate, the most lasting sex
possible. Only a God-ordained marriage makes this
all achievable, because one's success in sex is only
indicative of the kind of relationship they are in when
they are having it. A temporary relationship breeds
temporary pleasure. A codependent relationship brings
about a selfish sex life. A casual relationship simply
means that there are two people who do not take each
other's feelings or bodies very seriously. "Friends
with benefits" is a shorter way of saying, "I want the
gratification without the responsibility." That is not the
formula for a lasting friendship, whether it's in the bed
or out. As a matter of fact, none of these are.

I have actually had people ask me if I believed any
of the men in my past could have been my husband
if I had done things differently. Let me first say that
playing the "what if" game is a dangerous one, but I

will admit that when it comes to a couple of people,
if I had not picked the forbidden fruit before it had
ripened, our lives together may have been different —
sweeter instead of sour. This is where the first lesson I
learned about myself comes in. A "Mr." that comes into
your life may not be "Mr. Right," and he's certainly not
"Mr. Right Now." Either way, even the all-powerful
God chose to take seven days to create the earth.
When you meet a man, what's the rush? If he's yours,
he's not going anywhere, and if he leaves, or you find
yourself using some kind of elaborate scheme or tactic
to keep him there, he wasn't really yours to begin with.
Just because he may have taken what you had to offer
doesn't mean he belonged to you. It just meant he was
greedy. And while I'm on the subject, him leaving full
while leaving you depleted doesn't make him a dog;
it just makes you too giving — giving of something
he was never supposed to have in the first place.
The sad fact is, when you sleep with someone who is
not your lifetime companion, you are stealing from
them, and they are stealing from you, which severely
compromises the integrity of the relationship. For
a relationship to be morally stable, it has to have an
honest foundation.

I remember when Reggie, the father of my third
child, said something I wish I had heard years before
we met at that college party. "Shellie, even if I was
attracted to you, and even if there was a possibility
that we could be together, you told me you were cool
with our relationship as it was — as it had started. You
said you understood that although we had a sexual
relationship, I was going to remain with my girlfriend.
I couldn't trust you now if I wanted to, because you
lied. You didn't keep up your end of the bargain."

Cost-cutter copulation. There's nothing like it, but

he's right. He didn't do anything to me that I didn't let him do. I thought so little of myself that I didn't believe I deserved someone like him all to myself, so I settled for a part. You'll never be happy when you settle, because you were never created to have to do so. God saw me as a queen, not some carnal peasant girl. God is a supernatural visionary. Reggie was just a man. It was my job to open up his spiritual insight, not his carnal eyesight. It's hard for anyone to see the truest essence of your being in a dark room under cotton bed sheets.

But my problems began way before Reggie came along. Part of the reason why I shared brief excerpts of my childhood and adolescence was not to upset or humiliate anyone. It was to show you just how much your upbringing can affect you and how vital it is to get any issues you may have from your younger years resolved, or you may find yourself repeating them as an adult. For instance, if I had realized just how damaging my relationship with Melissa (my adversary) had been, there would've probably been no Dee Dee my freshman year in college, which means there would have been no David. Who knows how much pain I could have avoided if I had chosen the right kinds of friends—ones with awesome characters and not just great looks, ones who got attention for standing up for what was right and not laying down with all of the wrong people.

If I had found a way to fully reconcile with my mother before just a couple of years ago, perhaps the lives of my unborn children would have been spared, or better yet, the cycle of unwanted pregnancies would've ended. It wasn't just that the verbal, and at times physical, abuse I endured caused me to think lowly of myself, but as a direct result, I harbored fear, resentment, and bitterness in my heart, even when those in my life tried to make amends, as my mother did. Because of what had happened in my adolescence, I no longer trusted her, and because she was the first person I remembered trusting, she was the first person who I felt betrayed me. I was so hurt by what was lacking in our relationship that I never developed a real relationship with myself, which meant I didn't trust me very much either.

You don't really like people you don't trust. I didn't like my mom much. I didn't like me at all, so I couldn't even compute how to treat my children. In many ways, I felt like a dead woman walking on a daily basis, and I believed that by putting them to sleep, I was doing them a major favor. If I had accepted my mother's apologies a little sooner, if I had been open to understanding her pain that at times caused me to experience harm for which she never consciously intended, and if I had consulted God on how to forgive her and let the past go so I could see her present state, there's a great chance that my life would have been very different.. Showing someone how much they hurt you by hurting yourself only deepens the wounds and adds more time to the healing process. My children did not deserve to die just because I found myself having flashbacks of wanting to die myself at times as a child. My children deserved to see just how awesome of a woman—but more importantly, a mother, *my* mother, their grandmother—she had become. And most of all, my children and I deserved to see how awesome of a person I was becoming. My past did not have to dictate my future. With God, all things are possible.

With God, all things are possible. God, my Father. My Father. I didn't even know how to fully grasp that concept for quite some time, either. Growing up, to me, God was some guy I studied about in Bible class or talked about in Sabbath School, and that was cool, but if He was to serve as a father figure for my life, thanks, but no thanks. The first (earthly) father I had I only saw every summer for a few hours a day, and the second showed his love for me in the form of sexual abuse—not all of the time, but more than once, and even one time is more than enough. I had all of the "fathers" I could stand, and I think that's just the way the enemy wanted it to be. I had been a daddy's girl more than once, and it never lasted or worked out the way I planned or even the way I believe that God intended it to be.

As a young adult, I had no desire to have a dad literally, figuratively, or spiritually. Ladies, let me tell you something that will spare you from having to write some of my stories: We all need a daddy, in the sense that we all need our Heavenly Father, and it goes way beyond quoting hymns and memory verses in church. When you grasp hold of what God thinks of and feels for you, what He wants for your life, and what He will move heaven and earth to give you, you can't help but feel good about yourself. The enemy knows that, and that's why he tries to give us unhealthy images in our earthly fathers. It took me some time to say this and actually mean it, but I don't believe either of my fathers had malicious intent. They were hurting because of abuse and abandonment in their own childhood, and because they too did not "forgive and let go," they raised their own children with suppressed and unresolved feelings. You cannot correctly express love, even when you feel it, if you don't fully understand it. Sadly, during my childhood, they didn't. I hope God has shown them His love for even them now, for their sakes.

But remember, my childhood was only one chapter

in this book. There were other lessons that followed.
Another question I am often asked is if I regret not
being a virgin. Well, regret won't do me much good,
but I will tell you this: The unconditional loyalty I had
for my first, David, I find myself praying that God will
restore for the sake of my future lifetime companion.
Aside from the low self-worth issues, part of the reason
why I was so willing to overlook David's drug habits,
other women, police record, and violent temper, was
because I was bonded to him in a way I had never
experienced before and couldn't fully comprehend (see
what I mean about the power of sex). Like I said in
the very beginning, I had no plans of being with more
than one person, so even with all of the bad that came
along with being in a relationship with him, I assumed
I had to endure it because I belonged to him. The low
self-worth is what made me stick with the negative
aspects of the relationship, but the absolute devotion
I had for him came from what sex is created to do for
two people who love one another. As my mother often
says, "The rules of sex don't change just because the
circumstances do. Sex is meant to bond you to another
individual, another soul, another life." The difference
in a marriage is that it's for life.

I fear that a lot of us have become cynical about
our lifetime commitments because we have physically
bonded with so many others before. To this day, I have
male friends who are just as sexually active as they
were in college, and they're still complaining about the
same thing: "I slept with her one time, and suddenly
she's trippin'. She's calling all of the time like she's my
girl or something. It was just sex." I often tell these
guys that those kinds of girls are merely doing what
they were created to do when they give something that
was meant for one man to many. Women who bond

to guys after sex (and vice versa) are not extreme; the people who can sleep around and not care are. Remember that.

And because we are created to bond to those with whom we are physically intimate, if after doing so, we do not repent of our ways, we can often find ourselves creating a cycle. You couldn't have paid me to believe that I would have had numerous partners; that there would be times when I would be sharing men in every sense of the word; that I would actually have an instance when I didn't know who the father of my own child was; that I would go into debt financially and emotionally just so I could be kissed and cuddled; that I would get so good at lying that I would believe the lies myself; that I would willingly hurt other women — my sistahs — just to be with their male crushes, their boyfriends, and at one time, even someone's fiancé. But once sex was introduced into my life — once I found a distraction from the emotional pain I was experiencing, my drug of choice, so to speak — I didn't know how, and (this is key) I didn't want to learn how, to stop. So, I would use B to get over A and C to get over B. Soon I found myself with a lot of words with no meanings behind them. Trust me when I say that a man cannot heal your wounds; only God can, and when you're single, sex does not simplify; it only complicates — and in many cases, worsens — matters.

I'm not going to pretend the physical part doesn't have its perks, either. There's no way I'm going to sit here and act like the act of sex is horrible, 'cause it ain't. However, it is a temptation I will have to deal with for the rest of my life until I get married, and it didn't have to be that way; it's a temptation that can be avoided — and should be at all costs, because the price of pleasure is just too high when you're single, even if

you never have any obvious physical consequences.
You know how the Bible discourages us from worrying
about things in life (Matthew 6:25-34)? Well, I'm here
to tell you that there has not been one time after having
sex that I have not had to worry about something.
If it's not potential pregnancy, it's a potential health
risk. If it's not obsessing with how into a guy I am, it's
being consumed with how into me he's not. If it's not
spending days of my life that I won't get back getting
over the relationship, it's wasting countless days of
my life looking for the next guy to fill the void. If it's
not leaving me envious of the next girl, it's leaving me
paranoid about the last one. If it's not being at his beck
and call, it's trying to lose his phone number when
the affair comes to an abrupt end. It's just not worth
it. Looking back, there's not one guy I have told you
about, about whom I can say the sex was worth all that
comes along with it afterward, whether I liked him,
lusted him, or loved him. The temporary gratification
has too many long-lasting results; leave this book on
your nightstand for those times when your libido tries
to tell you otherwise.

But I didn't write this just to give you a variety of
reasons why you shouldn't have sex until marriage. I
also wrote this to share with you the pitfalls to look out
for when it comes to potential romantic relationships.
The most important—and I would think the most
obvious one—is to never date someone who is dating
someone else. Although I shared the reasons behind
why I did it, they weren't very good ones. Despite
what the media or myths may tell you, there is not
such a shortage of good men—or women—that you
have to share them with someone else. And no one is
complimenting you by being willing to let you be their
part-time interest. To be the one to whom they do not

commit, or acknowledge in public, as the person they are proud to be seeing, is the greatest insult; I don't care what they are telling you behind closed doors. All feet appreciate a doormat on which to wipe their feet. But while I'm at it, being a potential part-time lover isn't just about being a bed companion. Anytime you entertain more than platonic company with someone who is seeing someone else, you are skating on very thin ice. People who flirt with you while they are in a relationship don't respect the relationship or you—and never will—if you entertain that gobbledygook.

However, I personally believe many of us settle for less because either we don't know what we want, or we don't have enough patience to wait for what we desire. A wise woman once said that if you don't have a map, you don't know where you're going. I believe this applies to relationships. A lot of the trouble I got into was because I didn't have a trail map to guide me. I didn't take the time to compile a list of what I desired, and then ask God who would be the best companion for my life, so I could steer clear of the pitfalls. I'll show you what I mean.

If I had my list before meeting David—my first—I would have never gotten involved with him, because he would have been missing so many things that it would have prevented him from being more than a casual acquaintance. Believe me when I say that I would have never consciously gotten with a man who sold drugs, skipped school (high school at that), or cursed all authority figures, including his mother and the police. I would have never gotten involved with Michael, because aside from the fact that he had a girlfriend, he asked me to do things that were crass and personally disrespectful (like flashing him outside in a car). I would have never had sex with people who caused me to go into debt, or who I felt I had to lie to just to keep in my life. I would have never found myself sleeping with the fathers of my unborn children after the terminations. I would have never let a man call me out of my name (like the "B" word in anger or even in what he considered to be kinky sex), abuse my body under the guise of sexual enjoyment, or give him the power to control my self-perception. I would have never put myself in a place where I was kneeling down before them more than I was ever worshiping God. Bottom line, I would have never had to write this kind of book, because there would have been a different story to share.

But as God says, all things work together for good. It wasn't easy for me to share these things, but I do believe I was called to do so. Sadly, both in and out of the Church, these are not topics that are discussed nearly as much as they are happening. Sure, we touch on the spiritual laws and the physical consequences, but often our denial, our secrets, our ignorance, and our shame prevent us from practically applying God's Word to those who are affected by sexual misuse (any sex outside of God's intention). The sad fact is that many people are sexually active without understanding the physical, emotional, and spiritual risks. The sad fact is that many women are so concerned with what people will think about the physical evidence of their private lifestyles that children are aborted every single day. The sad fact is that many men are using sex to mask their own pain, but there are not enough qualified outlets to address these issues. The sad fact is that so many of us have been doing relationships wrong for so long that we believe what we are doing is right, or at least acceptable. The sad fact is that while no one really wants to talk about this stuff, it has to be talked about. All of it. Sure, the spiritual and physical consequences are vital, but the emotional ones can be just as deadly, which is a huge reason for my writing this. Many of us know we should wait, but I believe my story will give deeper insight into *why* we should wait. But I am not the only one with a story to tell. It has been my experience that wounds heal better when they are uncovered—that way they can breathe; far too many of us have skeletons in our closet that are haunting us; far too many of us are holding our things back, and it's killing us.

So, I'm sure you are wondering what ever came of my past when it comes to my present. In some cases, forgiveness and reconciliation were necessary, but when you are a recovering codependent, there is one thing you must keep in mind on your road to remission. I once heard a pastor say that while God wants your exes saved just as much as you may, that doesn't necessarily mean He wants you to do the saving. I couldn't have said it better. It took a long time for me to understand that letting go of the past often means I am not to hold on to people in my past, either. I believe that the story of Lot's wife looking behind her and turning to a pillar of salt as a direct result even applies today (Genesis 17:19-26). If you're not careful, the past can paralyze you. A part of the reason why I remained attached to people longer than the relationship, or "non-relationship relationship," lasted was because I didn't know how to let them go. One of my closest female friends used to call me the "girlfriend martyr" because I would try to be friends with those guys after things came to a head (the relationship came to an end)—or rather, after they showed their tail (I saw them for what they really were … bad for me).

"Shellie, a friend wouldn't do to you the things

that some of them did. Why do you even want to be associated with them?" she'd ask.

I'll tell you why. I didn't like myself enough to know that those guys should have taken some of the responsibility for the things that went wrong in the relationship. My friend was right. If people cannot esteem you, protect you, love you, and sustain you on a nonphysical level, you can never expect them to on an amorous basis. A friend is supposed to serve as a support system as you work toward becoming a better person. If after a relationship has ended, you find yourself worse off than you were before the relationship started, there is a good chance that person is not supposed to be in your immediate circle of emotional intimacy, and yet, so many of us try to make that be the case. Now, am I saying you can never be friends with someone with whom you have been immorally intimate? No. But what I am saying is that when you have been bonded to someone on an immoral level, integrity has to be restored before anything positive can come from it. The first thing many of us tend to do is jump right into a friendship because our residual feelings motivate us to do so. You can love them, but love them from a distance for a while. Remember the first word used to describe love in 1 Corinthians 13 is "patient." Be still and wait until God tells you what to do with those feelings. Trust me when I say that you are not qualified enough to figure it out all on your own. If you were, you wouldn't be in such a complicated predicament in the first place.

This point brings us back to me—and the things that went on inside of me. While I was still a virgin, I recall telling my mother, actually out of spite, that I was going to break the curse of sexual abuse and divorce in my home. It was my way of saying that since

everyone else was so "sick," I was going to make sure
I did whatever needed to be done to keep from being
as crazy as I thought they all were. Her immediate
response was, "Be careful. The enemy gets very angry
when you become bold enough to take on such a task."

Right again. There's not too much I haven't
experienced when it comes to the issue of sex, and
even now I am remaining prayerful of some of the
consequences that could come to haunt me. I'll give
you an example. There was a period of time after my
relationship with Chris (the last guy mentioned in this
story) that I was self-diagnosing what I believed to
be a yeast infection. After a few months of it getting
worse, I went to the doctor. It was then that I found
out I had a yeast infection that would not go away
because I had an untreated STD. Months and months
after being sexually intimate with Chris, I was still
paying for it dearly. After all of the other men I had
been with without contracting a disease, I figured
at least in this area I was invincible; when you are
operating outside of God's covering, that's never the
case. Thankfully, it was treatable, and the doctor says
I am healthy, but even after several years of making
mistake after mistake, I still had a lesson to learn.
Maybe, just maybe, this was the greatest one: Don't
get so caught up in how things look on the outside,
because it's what's on the inside that matters. I was so
obsessed with how men looked that I didn't notice how
ugly they were internally until it was too late. I was so
beaten up on the inside that I did all I could to make
sure the outside looked good to mask the pain. I was
so scared about looking pregnant that I didn't take the
time to accept the fact that on the inside, something
was growing with every breath I took. I was so caught
up in how relationships were looking to me on the

outside that I was literally willing to let other people's men be inside of me regardless of the circumstances or the consequences. And I let my outward conditions dictate my life for so long that I didn't even hear the words God was trying to speak to me concerning me and my self-worth.

"I've never quit loving you and never will. Expect love, love, and more love!" (Jeremiah 31:3, The Message).

"Don't be flip with the sacred. Banter and silliness give no honor to God. Don't reduce holy mysteries to slogans. In trying to be relevant, you're only being cute and inviting sacrilege" (Matthew 7:6, The Message).

just believe

Yeah, it's that simple
Why complicate your life with the things of this world
When you, yourself are not of it
Rise above it
To the vision that is before you
Can't you see
Before the womb, you were called and chosen
So, you have no other choice
Just believe
Just believe that your words can manifest miracles
For you are a child of the Creator
In seven days He spoke and it was so
So why do you doubt yourself
When you are a chosen vessel
A child of the King
His own Son said that you would perform greater things
Than even He
Just believe
Just believe that no mountain is too high
In the physical or the spiritual
Why try to climb what you can move
In the visual
Don't you know that faith is the evidence
of things not seen
A gift in the present
So, free your mind
With open arms
Ready to receive
Just believe
Just believe
Yeah, it's that simple
Just believe
You can manifest miracles
No mountain's too high

You're an eagle
Soar above your obstacles
And even higher to your dreams
And ultimately toward your destiny
The sky's the limit
Yeah, just believe

chapter eleven
inside my purpose

Do you know that throughout all of these experiences, initially, I rarely gave God a second thought? It wasn't so much that I was mad at Him or didn't love Him; it wasn't even that I doubted that I needed Him in my life. It was more like I didn't trust Him enough to go to Him. To me, all of the people I had loved and relied on in times of need had always vanished, and, considering the fact that I had never seen Him before, I figured, *What's the point in trying to get Him to look at me? What's the point in having Him see beyond the façade of my satisfaction into my hurt and pain — my sin?*

God is amazing. Although I couldn't see Him, He was always there. After every breakup, termination, and devastation, the presence of God was in my life, and He never came to my spirit with the judgmental fire and brimstone garbage that people in the Church wanted me to feel. Ironically, many times I steered pretty clear of anything that had to do with God — thinking religion was the key to making my relationship with Him work — because of the gossiping mouths or staring eyes of many who attended church in their Sabbath or Sunday best. Sure, I went to church. Sure, I said grace at the dinner table and led the family in prayer upon request. Sure, I could sing along with some of the most famous contemporary

Christian artists as my mother played them on the CD player in our home, but when it came to my own personal friendship with the Lord, I barely knew Him or believed I wanted to. Amazing how I was willing to endure all of the abuse from mere mortals, but was scared to take a chance on the only One who has never hurt me—the only One who was wholeheartedly committed.

But before I was conceived, God had a plan, so I had to get to know Him, even if I didn't know it at the time. Even in the midst of my mess, God had me turn to Him, and amazingly, initially, it was always in a way that was writing-related—a way that coincided with His purpose for my life. The path I was to take was going to be radical, so the journey had to match up. At first I was journaling out all of my feelings—not some poetic recitations that looked good on paper, but the filthy junk that'd make you think God would strike you down for even thinking it, let alone putting it into words. What we forget is that God knows what we are thinking anyway, and if death were the immediate result, we all would have been goners years ago.

"Tell me how you feel, Shellie," I would hear Him say. "Not how you think I think you feel, but how you really feel."

And I did. The good, the bad, the ugly, the uncensored, and when necessary, the R-and X-rated. For a while God was silent, but then after a couple of months, He said, "Now get a concordance and find out what the Word says about how you are feeling." Lord knows the last thing I wanted to do was read the Bible (because I didn't know how to personally apply it), but He also knew that I didn't want to stay in my emotional waste any longer. I began writing out my feelings in black ink and "His responses" via the Word in red. Soon we were dialoguing in a way I never had before, and God was revealing Himself to me in ways unimaginable to my broken spirit—not the "God" I heard about in private school or at church, but the God who loved me enough to create me and enough to keep me even when I was trying to destroy myself and those around me ... even when it was hurting Him to watch it all unfold.

When I was hurting from memories of my childhood abuse, He gave me Psalm 22: 24: "For He has not despised or disdained the suffering of the afflicted one; He has not hidden His face from him but has listened to his cry for help."

When I felt like He hated me because of my filthy lifestyle, He gave me Psalm 145:8: "The Lord is gracious and compassionate, slow to anger and rich in love."

When I was at my weakest as it related to temptation, He gave me James 4:7-8: "Submit yourselves, then, to God. Resist the devil and he will flee from you. Come near to God and He will come near to you ..."

When I battled with my conscience as it related to the sins I committed, He gave me Lamentations 3:31-33: "For men are not cast off by the Lord forever. Though He brings grief, he will show compassion, so great is His unfailing love ..."

When I pondered my existence, He gave me James 1:5: "Before the womb, you were called and chosen ..."

When I was scared to trust, He gave me Proverbs 3:5-6: "Trust in the Lord with all your heart and lean not on your own understanding; in all your ways acknowledge Him and He will make your paths straight."

When I was looking for clarity on my sexual desires,

He gave me 1 Corinthians 6:18-20: "Flee from sexual immorality. All other sins a man commits are outside of the body, but he who sins sexually sins against his whole body. Do you not know that you are the temple of the Holy Spirit, who is in you, whom you have received from God? You are not your own; you are bought at a price. Therefore honor God with your body."

Yes, He was speaking, but at first, I still wasn't listening. Not entirely. If I had been, there wouldn't have been so many chapters in this book. Even with all I was coming to know, I still wanted the physical presence of someone's love. I had heard people say they loved me before, while their actions said otherwise. How was I to be sure God wasn't just serving up some lip service as well, especially since He couldn't be seen with the physical eye? But He always came to me with statements and promises, and sadly, I always responded to Him with more questions and concerns (this only prolonged the process—that's what made it sad). Sure, the Scriptures sounded good, but for quite some time, that was about it.

I think I had my first real intimate experience with God on a one-on-one level when Damien died. I say this because, as I previously shared, over the last several months with Damien, there was barely any physical intimacy at all, although we had found ourselves growing closer than ever. After he passed, I believe that was God's way of saying, "You have mastered non-physical intimacy with a person. Now try it with me." And although I could conceptualize emotional intimacy without physical interaction at that point, because Damien was taken from me, I then feared God's permanence in my life. Would I fall in love with Him, only to have Him leave me too? I knew what His Word said would take to make Him happy, and I just wasn't sure if I was ready to make the sacrifice at this point. Again, more questions amid His promises. He was still working on me. He was still healing wounds.

I would love to say that what caused me to want to get closer to Him was His unbelievable forgiveness as it related to the loss of my unborn children, but to be honest, I was riddled with a lot of guilt for quite some time. Sure, He may not have struck me down with lightning, but I was willing to bet there would be punishment upon punishment lurking around the corner. For a long time, that is just how I lived my life—in a constant state of paranoia. Surely He wouldn't give me someone to love again. Surely whatever plan He had for my life would never come to pass because of all the wrong I'd done. Surely I would not be able to put the past behind me and was destined to be what people said I would become.

I had yet to see a lot of His words in action (to the physical eye, anyway), but I was living evidence of the manifestation of verbal abuse, taunts, and teases. Words do have life, and they do hurt, so I was not big on words at that point. But God never left my side, and when I look back, He was the only constant that always remained. Nothing shocked Him, nothing surprised Him, but like those closest to me, He was tired of seeing me hurt; tired of catching the blame for all of the bad things other people had done to me; tired of me giving to others what was meant for the one He destined for my life; tired of seeing me abort my children while believing the problem was the pregnancies and not the fornication and what led up to the act; tired of me getting with the same guy but in a different packaging year after year; tired of giving me promises of life as I contemplated death; tired of me not trusting in Him and the love He had for me.

As I have previously stated, it wasn't until the end of my relationship with Chris (the last person mentioned in this book) that I saw just how much the enemy hated me, but it also wasn't until then that I saw just how much God loved me and how much He was willing to move out of the way to give me what He thought I deserved.

And you know what? I now see that the devil knew my destiny, and he sent all of those men as distractions. He knew if I was caught up enough in what they saw, they said, they wanted, I would be too bruised, too damaged, too tired to do what I was placed on this earth to do—to break the curses I so boldly professed that I would just years before. He knew if I was consumed with gratifying my flesh—whether through self or at the hand of another—I wouldn't notice just how severely my spirit was harmed. And he knew if I defined love by what was modeled to me by man, I would never fully grasp what God had for me or just how perfect love could be.

God never intended for me to stress out in relationships. He never intended for me to chase, rather than be the one who was to be pursued. He never intended for me to go into financial, emotional, and physical debt while trying to maintain a relationship. He never intended for me to see my unborn children as a burden rather than a blessing. He never intended for me to have to share a man's affection or attention. He never intended for me to be unhappy—period. And He never intended me to over-spiritualize to the point that I would miss all of that. See, His words were not just words; they were written actions. Remember, He created the earth just by speaking. He was trying to recreate my world by doing the same. He was trying to show me what He had planted deep inside of me under all of the scars, the bruises, and the heartache way before anyone had harmed me.

Soon I was finding myself writing even more. My journaling turned into poetry, and my poetry into prose. Soon I was writing personal narratives and then sharing them with others. Through God's Word, I was discovering who I really was and sharing it with others. God was showing me I didn't need to be ashamed of my past, because after I repented, He didn't even acknowledge it, and in return, my experiences would be used to help others—somehow, some way. Everything was a step in the process, from the experiences, to the journaling, to the poetry, to my writing career, to this very moment. It wasn't just about telling a whole bunch of stories, but about sharing how I safely arrived at the final ending and letting people know that in it, I have found real happiness, real love, real peace. A real God, a real me.

Like me, you may have moments when you look in the mirror and you don't like what you see, and worse yet, you wonder how anyone else—including God—could either. Like me, you may have repeated some of the same mistakes because you thought bad love was better than no love, and being with anyone was better than being alone. Like me, you may have been so consumed with what was going on in the outside world that you missed out on what was going on inside of you. It's not a coincidence that you read my story, and it's not by chance that you are reading this chapter. I am living evidence of God's love and forgiveness, but also of His patience and His purpose. Even in the height of my tragedies, God's promises were for me. He still wanted me to know that He was merciful and compassionate and that I was called to do something great. He didn't need the opinions of those on the sidelines of my life. He didn't need the advice of the men from my past. He didn't even need the reservations I had about myself. He just needed me to be willing to look beyond what I saw in the physical sense and into His spiritual reality.

More than anything else you have read, I am most proud to say that even with all that has been taken from me—whether by others or my own hand— even now, God is in the process of restoration and preparation for the awesomeness that is to come; that although I have to stay on my knees daily to keep control over my flesh, in doing so, I have learned about real intimacy—Godly, healthy, lasting intimacy; that when I look in the mirror now, I like what I see. I have learned to rely on God's approval, not man's; that I am no longer "crazy, insane, or ridiculous," because in God, I am new and different creature, and I do new and different things; and finally, that even with all of the poor parenting decisions I made, I am not barren. God has planted something awesome inside of me that will play a part in birthing breakthroughs for others in their own relationships with God, others, and themselves.

You just finished reading it.

no more

No More
No more waking up in the morning
with my first priority not being prayer
No more setting the clock a half-hour early
to paint on features that ain't even there
No more skipping breakfast and picking up a biscuit
on the way to work; the time I spend at home
heating up my bagel I can be warming up my car, instead of
neglecting that necessity then wondering
why my car's running funny
No more walking in the office
with a nasty attitude reminiscing
of what happened the day before
No more clocking in five minutes late,
demanding more hours, getting rejected
and wondering why I'm poor
No more french fries at lunch instead of a salad,
Coke instead of water, candy instead of fruit,
and so then I won't have to complain
about why I am edgy, my face is splotchy,
or my waste line's pudgy
No more getting off and hitting up the cell
on the ride home, the fifteen minutes of solitude
would do me good; the messages can wait,
they're saved and this month's phone bill's been paid
No more making little stops
if they weren't planned ahead
No more going off in traffic jams, I know it's 5 p.m.,
I need to chill; I can't afford no accident
No more stopping by Tiger Mart for chips and a magazine
No more consulting Cosmopolitan without consulting my
conscience, I'm made distinctly;
J.Lo and Halle ain't got nothin' on me
No more depending on Mac or Crème of Nature
to define my beauty
No more envying the white girls' tresses,
the video hos dresses; true beauty can't be bought
with hair tracks, perms, artificial locs or push-up bras
No more letting someone else's insecurities intimidate me
No more apologetic explanations for my natural crop,

vintage style, full-lipped over-bitten smile; I'm realizin' the ones
criticizin' have been jockin' all the while
No more coming home to a mess house
including clothes not washed, bed not made, bills not paid
No more going straight to the idiot box or CD player
without thanking God for another day
No more showers in the evening;
I deserve a bubble bath
No more broken nails, chipped toe polish, ashy skin,
or missed verbal repetitions of "I'm Every Woman,"
"There's no one like me," "I have a prepared destiny"
No more spending quality time worrying
about who said what, who went where, or should I be there
No more giving what I don't want, second-guessing
answers to questions given by God
No more going into relationships, unprepared, unaware
No more being the ex-girlfriend martyr,
the co-dependent counselor, the jealous friend,
the one who offends, the manic, the workaholic, the sex
addicted, the suppressed gifted, the disrespected,
the doormat, or the openly rejected
No more holding grudges against those who have transgressed
No more failing already taken tests
No more waiting for my ship to come in
No more not learning how to swim;
and in the meantime, I'm treadin'
No more consulting Oprah before Scripture
No more depressing love songs
of prolonged relationships gone wrong
No more lying to myself or withholding the truth
No more regurgitation of the pain someone's caused
No more hurting and then healing up in the mall
No more entertaining your mess or creating my own
No more crying to God about consequences I've made
No more doubting after I've prayed
No more being around people who don't better who I am
No more idolizing the companionship of a man or children
No more suppressing my feelings for the fear of your offense
No more being ungrateful for the times when you have been
tolerant of my shortcomings, mistakes, aches, and pains
No more consciously repeating them again ...

and again ... and again
No more holding on to what ain't mine,
by time, riding the line of Christian love and self-abuse
No more expecting the same of you
No more giving God less than what He created
No more falling victim to my generational curses,
past soul ties, mental fears, or unanswered prayers;
I'm His creature, God said it, I believe it, that settles it
No more delaying what's mine
No more first expecting that Mr. Right should be fine
No more wanting what I won't give
No more settling for the conscious negative
No more merely existing, I'm ready to live!
No more comparing my financial wealth,
emotional stability, or relational progression by the latest couple
on the cover of In Style, Ebony, or Essence
No more succumbing to People's definition of the 25 Sexiest
No more helping a man cheat because of or on me
No more being a hypocrite to the teenage girl
or entertaining the hormonal boy; repetition's become a bore and
I'm a diva, what am I trippin' for?
And while I'm at it ...
No more sitting on the couch over sit-ups on the floor
No more buying a new dress before giving to the poor
No more accepting the reputation
or creating someone else's of being a whore
No more giving my all without expecting so much more
No more scratching the surface without touching the core
It's a new day and I know what I want, it's God's best, I won't
settle for less so
No more
No more
No more